Come to my Party

A complete guide to party-giving for children from 1 to 12

DELPHINE EVANS
Illustrated by Sheila Carter

Hutchinson
London Melbourne Auckland Johannesburg

Copyright © Delphine Evans 1986
Illustrations copyright © Sheila Carter 1986

All rights reserved

First published in 1986 by Hutchinson Children's Books Ltd
An imprint of Century Hutchinson Ltd
Brookmount House, 62–65 Chandos Place, Covent Garden, London WC2N 4NW

Century Hutchinson Publishing Group (Australia) Pty Ltd
16–22 Church Street, Hawthorn, Melbourne, Victoria 3122

Century Hutchinson Group (NZ) Ltd
32–34 View Road, PO Box 40-086, Glenfield, Auckland 10

Century Hutchinson Group (SA) Pty Ltd
PO Box 337, Bergvlei 2012, South Africa

Set in Plantin by BookEns, Saffron Walden, Essex

Printed and bound in Great Britain

British Library Cataloguing in Publication Data

Evans, Delphine
   Come to a party: a complete guide to party
   giving for children from 1 to 12.
   1. Children's parties
   I. Title
   793.2'1   GV1205

ISBN 0 09 163330 3

Contents

1	**General planning and preparation**	10
2	**Party for toddlers**	18
	Stamp and clap	20
	Knock at the door	21
	Around and around	21
	Round and round the garden	21
3	**Parties for 3s and 4s**	22
	Lollipop party – indoors	23
	Coloured lollipops	25
	Two lollipops	26
	Lollipop action rhyme	26
	Lollipop for my friend	27
	The lollipop bush	28
	Cat and mouse	29
	The hokey cokey	29
	Teddy Bears' Picnic – indoors or outdoors	31
	Hunt the jelly babies	33
	Ring-a-ring-a-roses	34
	Musical jumps	34
	Teddy action rhyme	35
	Grandmother's footsteps	35
	London Bridge	36
	The Grand Old Duke of York	37
	Extra games and things to do	38
	Pass the bag	38
	Birthday noise story	39
	Busy bees	39
	Farmer, Farmer	40

4 Parties for 5s and 6s   41

Clown party – indoors   42
Hello   46
Musical clown puppets   47
Noise story: Noddy the clown   47
Ruby ring   48
Chinese clown whispers   49
Action rhyme: Happy   50
Pop goes the weasel   50
Sing song: If you're happy   51

Yellow Party – indoors or outdoors   52
Woolly fun   54
Giant's treasure   54
Oranges and lemons   55
Wobbling yellow jellies   56
Magic carpet   56
Fly away   57

Extra games and things to do   58
Spoon and sweets race   58
Pass the clothes   58
Creepy crawlies   59
Ten green bottles   59
Finger puppets   60

5 Parties for 7s and 8s   61

Balloon party – indoors   62
Competition: Money box   65
Balloon battle   65
Second-hand shop   66
Don't drop a balloon   66
Musical pillows   67
Rocket race   67
Sweet bashing   68
Noise story: the balloon shop   68
Burst the balloon   69

Animal party – indoors or outdoors	71
Competition: What's inside?	74
Animal team game	75
Bunny hops	76
Dead lions	77
Lap it up!	77
Noise story: Polly Parrot and Cyril	78
Animal talk	79
Danger zone	79
Old MacDonald	80
Extra games and things to do	81
Blow the feather	81
Run for the tumbler	81
Flour mountain	82
Pick a pea	82
Try a tongue twister	82

6 Parties for 9s and 10s   83

Card party – indoors	84
Competition: Eight eights	86
What card am I?	87
Hunt the cards	87
Throwing cards	88
Grab the Joker	88
Find the ace	89
Swop shop	90
Tied up in knots	91
Sports party – outdoors	93
Competition: Name that face	97
Balloon race	97
Pancake race	98
Four-legged race	98
Handicap Football	99
Tortoise race	100
Cock fighting	100
Buckets game	101

Extra games and things to do   102
Treasure hunt   102
Pull the ball   103
Animal pairs   103
Stepping stones   104
Jump the stick   104

7   Parties for 11s and 12s   105

Rainbow party – indoors   106
Competition: Who is it?   108
Rainbow tissues   108
Musical colours   109
Shoe fly   109
Rainbow Parade   109
Paperclip race   110
Eye witness   110

Bar-B-Q party – outdoors   112
Competition: Best in the West   114
Follow the string   115
Slap Jack   115
Brimming over   116
Pass the bridle   116
Burst the balloon – challenge   117

Extra games and things to do   118
Give and take   118
Hanky hockey   118
Don't giggle   119
Jumble sale   119
Dusty miller   120
Musical statues   120

8   General planning and preparation for large parties   121

9 Large parties for all occasions 127

Christmas 128
Easter 130
Hallowe'en 133
Street 137
Any other time 140
Games and things to do 141
Action rhyme: Christmas pudding 141
Action song: Here we go round the Christmas tree 142
Chickens for sale 143
Dunking for apples/marshmallows/buns 143
Musical numbers 143
Beanie 144
Hares and hounds 144
Letters 144

1
Before You Begin

General Planning and Preparation

So, you've decided to have a party. Relax – make up your mind it's going to be fun and that you're going to enjoy it as much as the children. You *can* do this, if you make your plans well in advance and take it in easy stages. Let the 'party person' be involved as much as possible from the beginning.

When is it to be?

The best time, of course, is on the actual birthday. Although, if this falls at an inconvenient time, you might prefer to wait until the following weekend or the school holidays. You could then have an outing to a cinema, pantomime, swimming pool, museum or zoo. Alternatively, arrange a ramble or nature walk.

How many are you going to invite?

This is bound to cause a great deal of discussion. There will be 'best friends' and those who 'must come, because I went to theirs'. The party person may even want to invite the whole class at school!

This is where you *must be firm*. Only invite as many as you can easily cope with in the space you have – either in your own home or in a small hall. Perhaps you might want to limit it to two or three for a special outing.

Where are you going to hold the party?

This will almost decide itself once you know the number of guests. Your home is probably easiest, providing you have enough space to clear the deck for games in one room and eat in another. Alternatively, use your garden and/or garage and make packed lunches/teas which can be eaten indoors or out according to the weather. Think also about parks, picnic areas and beaches.

What time of day?

Morning, afternoon or early evening? This will probably depend on the age group. Under-fives usually get a 'low' around lunchtime, so avoid this if possible. By far the best time for under-fives seems to be a 3.00 or 3.30 start. For children from six to ten a picnic lunch, fish and chips or bangers and mash party can be fun during school holidays. Early evening for nine to twelves will make it seem more grown up.

How long should it last?

Here again the age of the guests should decide the length of the party. For the very young, one and a half hours will be long enough – gradually extending to three hours for ten to twelve years olds. It's best to end before anyone becomes too tired or bored. If they want to continue when it's time to go home, then your party will have been a success.

Decide whether you will be collecting or delivering your guests. This is sometimes a good idea, as then no one arrives too early or stays too late.

Invitations

You now have enough information to write out your invitations. When – where – start – finish. It's fun to make these yourself, particularly as an invitation is the first indication of how good your party is going to be. The wording will be something like this:

> Dear ....
> I will be having a .... party, on .... at ....from .... until .... Please let me know if you can come.
>   (Love) from ....

Or if parents are being invited:

> Dear Jane and her Mum (or Dad) . . .

Add any other necessary information:

> We will collect you at .... We will take you home afterwards. Will you please bring your wellies and a warm coat. It will be a .... party so please wear ....

(More about clothes in the following chapters.)

Note: Buy your envelopes before you start to make your cards. If you do it the other way round, you could have difficulty finding envelopes of the correct size.

When do you send the invitations? At least two weeks before the party date.

How? Posting is probably safest, unless you can deliver each invitation personally to the child's home. Even important party invitations get lost, or forgotten, by children until the day before.

Expense

It's wise to give yourself a budget and stick to it, so make out a list of essential things you will need to buy. Your own particular talents will decide what you want to make and what will have to be bought. Adaptable suggestions for things which you and the party person can make are given later in the book, to tie in with the party themes. Remember to allow yourself plenty of time for this.

Professional entertainers

Names and addresses of entertainers can be found in local papers or the yellow pages, but make sure you ask about their fees. They could be the most expensive part of your party. Why not try some do-it-yourself entertainment instead?

Food

Most food can be cooked in advance and frozen – even the completed party cake can be 'open frozen' on a baking tray. (Remember to make a list of what you have put in the freezer.) Sandwiches can be prepared the night before and covered in cling film. Next day they can be cut into small bite-size pieces. Even older children like them this way and it avoids leftovers with just a bite missing! Bite-size small cakes are also popular, as are crisps, potato rings, savoury snacks, small biscuits, sausages on sticks, and fruit salad on sticks.

Try cheese on toast cut into small pieces and served warm. Small open sandwiches are a nice change: try sweet ones as well as savoury – sprinkling demerara sugar, hundreds and thousands or chocolate vermicilli on thin bread and butter.

Make flowers from star-shaped biscuits with a sweet in the middle. Give the biscuits a cocktail-stick stem and make the flowers 'grow' from half oranges.

Jelly with a difference: line the bottom of the mould with jelly babies or jelly sweets before pouring on the cooled jelly.

Try mini hot dogs – have a squeezy ketchup bottle handy.

Drink

Fizz up plain squashes with tonic water. Crush ice to make the drinks 'tinkle'. Make milk shakes and float ice cream on top for a special treat.

The party cake

Simple ideas are the most effective (and easiest). You don't need fancy moulds – it's surprising what you can do with a Swiss roll and plain sponges. Fudge icing will hold sweets and decorations better than glacé icing. You can paint food colouring straight on to glacé icing with a paintbrush. Lots of different decorations can be bought as well as fondant icing which you only have to roll out. Ideas for cakes are given in each chapter.

Prizes

Many small items can be purchased, but you will find ideas throughout the book for things to make.

Suggested prizes are note pads, pencils, unusual rubbers, badges, finger puppets, plastic jewellery, small farm animals, false noses, moustaches or lips, pencil sharpeners.

Work out how many you will need and then buy one extra, just in case.

Team prizes can be sweets, lollipops or other small items.

Note: Watch out for 'the clever one' who wins too often. Ask her/him to help you with one or two games. This will give the others a chance and make the clever one feel important.

Presents

Trends come and go, but your child will know what's 'in' or 'out'. A small gift to take home is a pleasant way of saying goodbye – especially if it fits in with the party theme. If you're having quite a few paper and pencil games, why not buy a wipe-off pad for each person to use and then take home. Otherwise, keep the going-home presents well hidden, as a final surprise.

Presents given to party person

Although children will want to open presents as soon as they are given, it's far better to wait until everyone has gone home. Decide this before the party and remember to mark the donor's name on the outside – just in case they didn't! Put the presents safely away (out of sight – out of mind). Thank you notes can be given out the next day, following this format:

    Dear ....
    Thank you for ....
        (Love) from ....

Help

How much are you going to need? This will depend on your own capabilities. Usually the younger the children, the more help is necessary. Someone may need to be taken home, want to go to the toilet in the middle of a game, feel sick, need a cuddle . . .

If you have too much help, your helpers may end up having their own tea party! So make sure you have people you know will actually help, and allocate them specific jobs. One might like to take photographs which will serve as a record of the party for you and the guests. It's cheaper to have extra prints developed at the same time.

Music

You will probably need music of some kind. Records or cassettes are the easiest as you can choose the music beforehand and have it ready. Otherwise an adaptable friend who plays guitar or piano may be happy to oblige. You can manage without music for most of the well-known singing games, and whistles, bells or gongs can be used quite effectively. Remember to warn the neighbours!

Safety

You will be busy and cannot be expected to have your eyes everywhere, so be extra cautious. The following list of safety rules is a good guide, but locations differ and you may need to add some of your own:

Inside

- Guard all fires – no matter what the age group.
- Roll up any loose rugs.
- Keep stairs clear.
- Lock up pills and medicines, disinfectants, bleach, etc.
- Keep pets away from the party. Even reliable ones can become frightened and some children do not like animals.

- Put away precious ornaments and toys.
- Have sticking plasters ready for minor accidents.
- Check electric plugs and loose wires. Young children love poking things into holes and pulling wires.
- Remove all door keys. Children love to fiddle and can easily lock themselves in.
- Lock outside doors to prevent young escapees but keep keys immediately accessible in case of fire.

Outside
- Keep outside gates closed and put a heavy obstacle against them if the latch does not work.
- Water can be dangerous – a child can drown in water which is only 5 cm deep, or slip on damp ground.
- Lock and remove key from garden shed and pack away machinery.

Garage
- This will need really thorough checking for chemicals and tools. If you are going to use one for the party it should be *empty*.

Make lists

Don't rely on your memory. Make lists and check them regularly. List guests – food and drink – cutlery – crockery (plastic or paper) – tablecloth (plastic or paper), a polythene sheet for under the table may be necessary – prizes and presents – props for games and decorations.

Final check

Make this the day before. Have you got everything on the list ready?

Party morning

Prepare rooms and decorations. Lay table. Mix drinks. Put food on table and cover if necessary. Make sure hot food is ready to cook or warm up. Put music ready. Have whistle, gong or bell handy in case your voice gives out. Put props and prizes easily accessible to *you*.

Golden rules

- Be well prepared.
- Provide plenty to drink – children have a great thirst.
- Plan extra games (just in case).
- Have lots of absorbent cloth handy.
- Keep a 'sick' bowl nearby.
- Show everyone where the toilet is. (Have spare pants available for younger children.)
- Don't put out too much food at a time. (This will ensure that most dishes are finished up.)
- Relax and enjoy it!

After the party

– Feet up – it's all over!
– Clear up sometime.
– Help party person open presents and fill out thank you cards.

Next day

Give out thank you notes and accept congratulations for a super party!

2
Party for Toddlers

Theme: Any chosen colour
(1–1½ hours)

Toddlers to be accompanied by an adult.

Invitations

Materials
Thin card ⎫ Either card or felt tip should be in the party
Felt tips ⎬ theme colour
Envelopes ⎭

Fold the card and cut to fit the envelope. Using the felt tip, draw a large 1 or 2 on the front of the card, and inside write the invitation: 'Sam and his Mum/Dad invite Sally and her Mum/Dad . . . etc. (See Chapter 1.)

Decorations

The guests will have a grown up with them, and may be too young to wear a badge, so make badges for adults, with child's name included. Get badges of the theme colour from a stationers, or use white badges with coloured felt-tip writing. Examples: 'Tony and Beth', 'Mary and Beth'.

Write the guests' names on paper napkins in the party theme colour, and use them as place name-markers.

Cake

Make the cake in the birthday number shape – 1 or 2. Bake 1 in an oblong tin and trim to shape. Bake 2 in two sections, round and oblong; cut and place together.

Ice in the theme colour with matching candle(s) if possible. (See illustration on page 20.)

Food

Keep all food in bite-size pieces.

PROGRAMME

Have toys available to play with and books to look at in between a few games, action rhymes and nursery songs which will be played by mother/father and child.

Stamp and clap – action rhyme

Stamp, stamp, stamp,
Upon the ground.
    (*Stamp up and down.*)

Clap, clap, clap,
And turn around.
    (*Clap and turn around.*)

Stretch, stretch, stretch,
Towards the sky.
    (*Stretch upwards.*)

Slap, slap, slap,
Upon your thigh.
    (*Slap thighs and start again.*)

Knock at the door

Knock at the door.
    (*Tap forehead.*)
Ring the bell.
    (*Pull a lock of hair.*)
Lift up the latch
    (*Pull nose.*)
And walk in!
    (*Open mouth and 'walk' fingers in.*)

Around and around – action rhyme

(*Do as the rhyme suggests.*)

Run around,
Run around,
Run, run, run.

Dance around,
Dance around,
Fun, fun, fun.

Turn around,
Turn around,
Done, done, done.

Round and round the garden

Round and round the garden
    (*Adult moves finger round toddler's hand.*)
Like a teddy bear.
One step, two step,
    (*'Walk' fingers up toddler's arm.*)
Tickle you under there.
    (*Tickle under arm.*)

3
Parties for 3s and 4s

Lollipop Party
(2 hours) *Indoors*

Invitations

Materials
Thin card
Envelopes
Felt tip or biro
A lollipop for each invitation

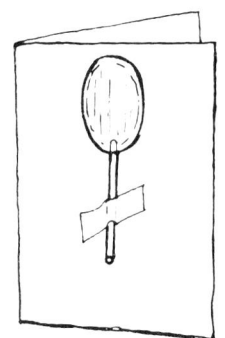

Cut out a piece of card which when folded in half lengthwise will fit your envelope. Attach the lollipop to the front and write the invitation inside. (See Chapter 1 for suggested wording.)

Make extra ones and keep for thank you cards. You could, if you prefer, *draw* a lollipop on the front of these.

Decorations

Materials
Cord or string
Paper or card
(all colours)
Tissue paper

Make three large card lollipops, one for the front door, and two to be used as puppets (see *Entertainment*, page 27). Make smaller ones to hang around the room. Cut out lollies from tissue paper and attach to windows for a pretty effect.

Name badges

Materials
Round cardboard badges (from stationers)
Straws
Coloured felt tips
Glue

Write a child's name on each badge, and glue on a length of straw to form the 'stick'. If possible, use a different coloured felt tip pen to write each guest's name (or different coloured badges). Use the same colour combination for name badges and place labels. This will make it easier for the children to find their places.

Place markers

Materials
Coloured card
Coloured felt tips
Potatoes
Cocktail sticks
Silver foil

Cut out a coloured card circle and write the child's name on both sides. Blunt one end of the cocktail stick and split down a short way. Place the circle in the split. Cover a piece of potato (3–4 cm square) with silver foil and push the sharp end of the cocktail stick into it.

If the guests cannot read their own names, you can make a good game of trying to match place markers to the writing and colour of their name badges.

Cake

Buy or make a round sponge for the lollipop, and use small chocolate-covered baby Swiss rolls for the lollipop stick (warm the ends and they will stick together). Cover sponge in glacé icing (bought or home-made) and swirl different food colours on with a paintbrush. Glue the 'stick' to the 'lollipop' with icing.

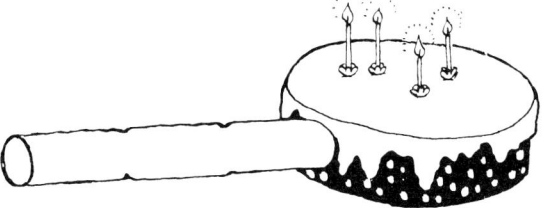

Food

Cut as much as possible into small pieces.

PROGRAMME

Coloured lollipops

Props
Music
Hanging lollipops. Use the lollipop decorations for this or make some large ones and suspend them from the ceiling – one or two in each of the primary colours.

Get the children to dance, jump or skip to the music and tell them that when it stops you are going to call a colour, e.g. 'red lollipops'. They will then have to find a red lollipop and stand under it. No winners or losers – just fun.

Two lollipops

Props (to be prepared before the party)
Coloured card lollipops about 10 cm long – enough for each child to have three pairs of different colours. These are simply made by drawing the lollipops on card and cutting out.
A bag for each child. Put three lollipops of different colours (half each of the child's three pairs) into each bag.

On the day
Spread all the loose lollipops around the floor. Give the children their bags and tell them to look inside, and then to find and pick up three more lollipops the same as the ones inside their bag.

Give a small prize to everyone who gets it correct.

Lollipop action rhyme
(*Children standing.*)

Five fat lollipops, juicy and sweet.
   (*Hold up one hand, fingers spread.*)
Five fat lollipops, nice to eat.
Lick – lick – lick,
   (*Pretend to lick one.*)
Throw away the stick.
   (*Pretend to throw away and hide one finger.*)

Four fat lollipops, juicy and sweet . . .
   (*Hold up four fingers, and continue in this way until:*)

No fat lollipops, juicy and sweet.
   (*Show fist.*)
No fat lollipops left to eat!
   (*Pretend to cry.*)

Repeat once or twice.

Lollipop for my friend

Props
One lollipop

The children make a circle, holding hands. Choose one child to be outside the circle and give her/him the lollipop to hold. Those left in the circle close their eyes and the lolly holder runs around the outside, whilst everyone sings to the tune of 'I sent a letter to my love':

I sent a lolly to my friend and on the way I dropped it.
One of you has picked it up and put it in your pocket.

The child on the outside has to run round the circle singing 'It isn't you – it isn't you. . . ' until (s)he drops the lolly behind someone, when (s)he says, 'It *is* you.' The children can then open their eyes to see if the lolly is behind them. Whoever finds it behind them has to pick it up and chase around the circle after the first child. The one who reaches the vacant space in the circle first is the winner and the other one has to run round the outside with the lollipop.

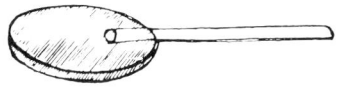

Toilet trip and wash hands ready for tea

*

Tea

*

Entertainment. Draw faces on your two 'puppet' lollipops. Use them to tell jokes, sing songs, recite rhymes – the guests joining in.

The lollipop bush

The children join hands in a circle and sing to the tune of *Here we go round the mulberry bush.*

Chorus
Here we go round the lollipop bush,
The lollipop bush, the lollipop bush.
Here we go round the lollipop bush,
On a cold and frosty morning.

Verses
This is the way we pick a lollipop,
    (*Pretend to pick a lollipop from the bush.*)
Pick a lollipop, pick a lollipop.
This is the way we pick a lollipop,
On a cold and frosty morning.

This is the way we eat a lollipop . . .
    (*Eat it, continue as first verse.*)

This is the way we get sticky hands . . .
    (*Wriggle fingers as if sticky.*)

This is the way we wash them clean . . .
    (*Wash them.*)

This is the way we sit down for a rest . . .
    (*Sit down.*)

Cat and mouse

Props
Music

The children scuttle around the floor on their hands and knees, squeaking, while the music plays. Stop the music and meow loudly. You can now play in one of two ways:

1 They must stay quiet and still, otherwise they are out of the game.
2 They must run off to a corner which is their home, before the 'cat' can catch them.

Repeat *Lollipop action rhyme*. This time they will remember it and it will be great fun.

The hokey cokey

Finish your party with this action song. The children stand in a circle.

First verse
You put your right arm in,
  (*Stretch right arm into circle.*)
Your right arm out,
  (*Right arm back behind you.*)
In – out – in – out,
  (*Right arm in and out.*)
Shake it all about.
  (*Shake it.*)
You do the hokey cokey and you turn around.
  (*Turn around.*)
That's what it's all about.
  (*Clap hands.*)

Chorus: (*Join hands and walk to middle of circle, gradually lifting arms above your head as you go, then walk back again, lowering your arms.*)

Oh hokey hokey – cokey.
Oh hokey hokey – cokey.
Oh hokey hokey – cokey.
That's what it's all about.
  (*Clap hands.*)

Verses
You put your left arm in . . . (*Repeat as first verse above.*)

You put your right foot in . . . (*Repeat as above.*)

You put your left foot in . . . (*Repeat as above.*)

You put your right side in . . . (*Repeat as above.*)

You put your left side in . . . (*Repeat as above.*)

You put your whole self in . . . (*Jump into circle – repeat as above.*)

Take home

Give each child a lollipop to take home.

Teddy Bears' Picnic
(2 hours) *Indoors or outdoors*

Invitations

Materials
Thin coloured card
Felt tip pen
Envelopes

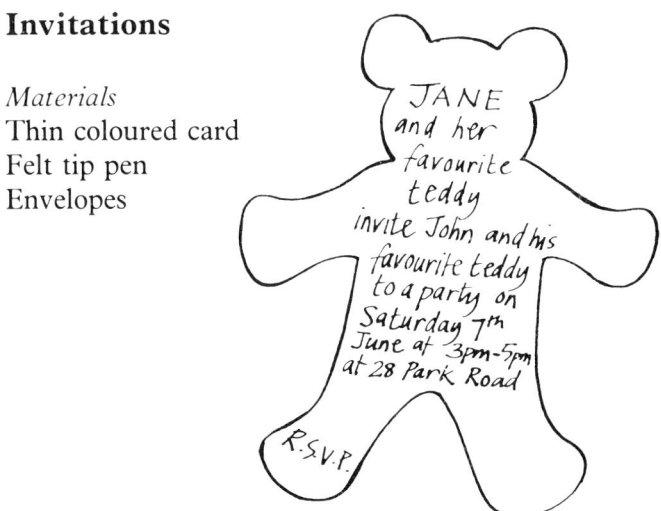

Draw a simple teddy bear design to fit your envelope. Cut it out, and use it as a pattern or template to make all the invitations you need, drawing round your shape and cutting each teddy out. Write your invitation on the front:

> Jane and her favourite teddy, invite John and his favourite teddy ... (See Chapter 1 for suggested wording.)

Make extra ones for thank you cards.

Decorations

Materials
Large piece of coloured paper or card

Cut out a large teddy for the front door or garden gate.

Name badges

Materials
Blank self-adhesive labels
Felt tips

Write the child's name on one and 'John's teddy' on the other – with either the label colour or the felt-tip colour matching. This will help if a teddy gets lost!

Cake

Buy or make a round sponge cake and cover it in fudge icing. Outline a teddy bear in sweets or decorate it with bought chocolate teddies.

Food

Separate food packs in paper bags are easy to prepare and fun to open. Write each child's name on the outside (this will avoid confusion if the child puts it down). Use felt tips in colours to match the name badges, or stick another coloured label on the bag. Don't put in too much, but provide some extras when the bags are empty.

Suggested contents
Small sausages, a packet of crisps, a couple of biscuits, a piece of cheese (wrapped in cling film) and a piece of fruit.

Make sure the children stay seated whilst they eat. Put drinks in small plastic bottles (provided you can save enough).

Shoe boxes, or small boxes about shoe-box size, make good 'lunch boxes' as an alternative to the food pack bags. You could even thread thick cord handles through each end as shown here.

Seating

Use a large rug or blanket for the picnic, which can be indoors or outdoors. Have an extra rug for teddies to sit on when they are watching some of the games.

PROGRAMME

Hunt the jelly babies

Props
3 or 4 jelly babies for each child

Preparation before the party
Place the jelly babies around the room (or in small paper cases around the garden).

On the day
Tell the children to hunt for the jelly babies. When they find one they can eat it – *but they must stand still* until they have finished it. This will give everyone a chance of success.

The teddies can help the children to play this game.

Ring-a-ring-a-roses

Form a circle with a teddy bear between each pair of children, all holding hands. Sing this song. Repeat the actions for verses two and three.

Ring-a-ring-a-roses,
   (*All stand in circle.*)
A pocket full of posies.
   (*Skip around holding hands.*)
A tishoo, a tishoo,
We all fall down.
   (*All fall down.*)

The king has sent his daughter
To fetch a pail of water.
A tishoo, a tishoo,
We all fall down.

The robin in the steeple
Is singing to the people.
A tishoo, a tishoo,
We all fall down.

Musical jumps

Props
Music

If you can't get music outside, use a whistle, gong or bell to stop the jumping.

Tell the children to put teddies on their rug to watch them play this game. The children jump up and down to the music. When it stops (or when the whistle is blown) they must stop jumping and stay perfectly still. Those who move are out of the game and must go and sit with the teddies.

Teddy action rhyme
(*For children and teddies, all standing.*)

Me and my teddy – like to jump about.
  (*Jump.*)
Me and my teddy – like to give a shout.
  (*Hold teddy up and shout, 'Hi!'*)
Me and my teddy – like to stamp our feet.
  (*Stamp.*)
Me and my teddy – like to take a seat.
  (*Sit down.*)
Me and my teddy – like to hop and hop.
  (*Hop.*)
Me and my teddy – like to stop, YES, STOP!
  (*Stop.*)

Toilet trip and wash hands ready to eat
*
Picnic time
*

Grandmother's footsteps
(*With teddy.*)

The children stand in a line with their teddies. You or another child must stand some distance ahead, with your back to them. You are Grandmother and they must creep up on you, but at any time you can spin around to catch them out. They must then stand still. If you see anyone move they must go back to the beginning (or out of the game). If anyone reaches you they can be Grandmother and all the others join in the game again.

London Bridge is falling down
(*Teddies to watch.*)

Two children or adults stand with arms raised, hands clasped together to form a bridge. The other children skip under quickly to get through the bridge before it falls down, and everyone sings:

London Bridge is falling down,
 Falling down, falling down.
London Bridge is falling down,
 My fair lady.

Build it up with silver and gold,
 Silver and gold, silver and gold.
Build it up with silver and gold,
 My fair lady.

As each child is caught by the arms of the bridge, he or she joins one of the lines behind the two who are forming the bridge. At the end of the game the two teams have a tug-of-war.

Repeat action rhyme

Tell them to go and find their teddies, because the teddies have told you they enjoyed the action rhyme so much they want to do it again. This time they will probably remember most of it and it will be great fun!

The Grand Old Duke of York

Grand finale with teddies and children marching up and down the lawn or room, singing:

The Grand Old Duke of York,
He had ten thousand men.
He marched them up to the top of the hill
And he marched them down again.

When they were up they were up.
When they were down they were down.
And when they were only half way up –
They were neither up nor down!

Repeat once or twice, according to energy!

Take home

Before the guests go home, tie a balloon to each teddy's arm.

Extra Games and Things to Do

Pass the bag – game
(*Play this before teatime.*)

Props
Music
A number of paper bags (various sizes and colours)
Rubber bands (optional)

This is a simple version of pass the parcel, made easier for young children.

Preparation before the party
Put three dolly mixtures (or similar) into the smallest paper bag. Tie, twist or put a rubber band around the top. Put this bag inside another, plus three sweets, twist top.

Continue in this way at least seven or eight times, according to the size of the party and age of the children. You will need a bag for each child.

On the day
Sit the children in a circle and explain what they have to do when the music stops, i.e. whoever is holding the bag opens it, takes out the bag inside and finds three sweets. He eats one himself and gives one each to the children either side of him to eat. When the music restarts, the bag is passed on.

Start the music. Watch that everyone gets a turn at opening the bag.

Birthday noise story

An adult reads the story and the children make the sound effects. Practise a few noises first – knock on door ....., whistle ....., fire engine ...., etc.

Today is [the party person's] birthday. He/she is ..... years old, so we clap .... times.
 The postman is coming up the path. He opens the gate .... knocks on the door .... and says, 'Happy Birthday'.
 At last the guests arrive for the party and .... opens his/her presents ..... He/she finds a drum ....., a whistle ....., a fire engine ....., a doll that cries ..... and a book about a dog ..... .
 They all play games which make them laugh ..... and shout ..... .
 The next game is with balloons, which they have to blow up ..... and then sit on until they pop ..... .
 Time for tea and it looks good, with jelly to eat ....., juice to drink ..... and a cake with candles on – which they have to blow out ..... one at a time ..... .
 The party ends with everyone singing, 'Happy Birthday .....'.

Busy bees – game

The children find partners and spread themselves out all over the room, with you, the Queen Bee (or King Bee!), standing in the middle.
 You then call out different things for them to do like, 'Jump up and down', 'Stand back to back', 'Hold hands and turn around', 'Skip'. They do this until you call, 'Buzz, buzz, busy bees', when they must all start buzzing and looking for a new partner. At the same time you must try to find a partner, although they must try to stop you finding one!
 The one left without a partner becomes the Queen or King Bee.
 If there is an odd number of children you can either enlist the aid of one of your helpers, or get the party person to be the first Queen/King Bee.

Farmer, Farmer – game

This game can be played either indoors or out of doors provided there is a space large enough for the farmer's field.

All the children stand in a row at one end of the 'field', which can be a lawn or a room, while the Farmer stands at the other end of his/her field.

All the children ask the Farmer politely:

'Farmer, Farmer, may we cross your field?'

The Farmer replies:

'Not unless you have ..... on,' and names a colour.

Those children lucky enough to have that colour on may then cross the field in safety, but the others are chased by the Farmer. If he catches them, he puts them in a 'pen' while the game continues with the rest of the children crossing backwards and forwards across the field, asking the same question, but getting a different colour in answer each time.

When only one child is left, he/she becomes the Farmer and the fun starts all over again.

4
Parties for 5s and 6s

Clown Party
(2 hours) *Indoors*

Invitations

Materials
Thin card
Envelopes
Sequins/glitter, sticky shapes, wool, etc., to decorate

Cut out a paper hat shape to fit your envelope and use as a template.

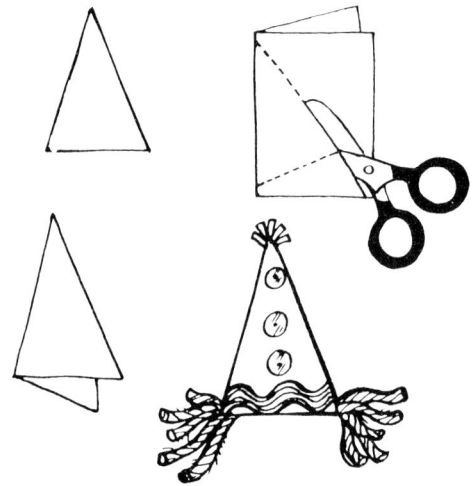

Cut out a piece of card and fold in half. Line up your hat template so that the edge of your card is along one side of the hat. Cut out the hat shape. Decorate with sequins, shapes, wool, etc., and write your invitation inside. (See Chapter 1 for suggested wording.)

Make extra ones for thank you cards.

Decorations – clown faces

Materials
Paper plates
Coloured paper
Paints/felt tips
Sequins/glitter, sticky shapes, wool, etc., to decorate

Decorate the paper plates to look like clowns and hang around the room. Keep one for the front door and make him a paper body and hat.

Rosette name badges

Materials
Round cardboard badges (from stationers)
Tissue paper
Glue
Felt tip pen

Cut strips of tissue paper, wrinkle them up and glue them around the edge of the badge.
  Write on the name.

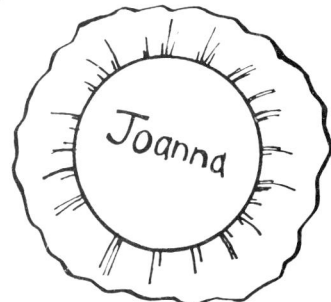

Clown place markers

Materials
Thin card
Felt tips

Cut out a piece of card 10 cm square. Mark a half-way line and draw a clown as shown – making sure that the hat starts on the line.

Write on the child's name.

Cut along the two sides of the hat and fold the card in half as shown, so that the hat sticks up.

Cake

Here are two suggestions.

Clown
Buy or make a round sponge and decorate with a clown's face, using either piped icing or a paintbrush dipped in food colouring.

Big Top
Put a knitting needle in the centre of a round sponge cake and attach ribbons to outside of cake board.

Draw out a pretend circus ring and decorate with animals.

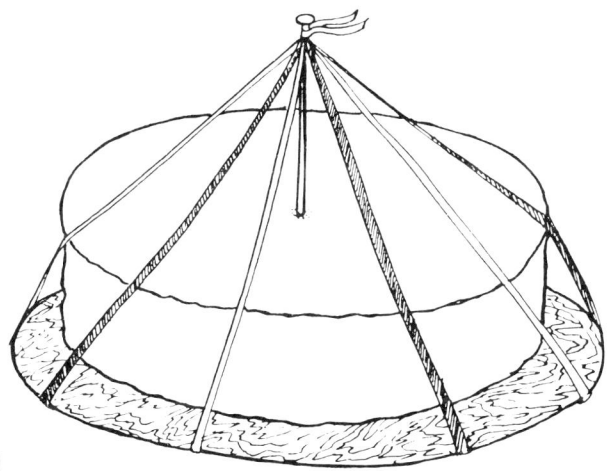

Food

Small cakes or biscuits can be decorated with happy clown faces. If you have animal biscuit cutters you can make circus animals, or buy ready made biscuit or chocolate animals.

Ice cream and jelly clown
Put the jelly in individual bowls/paper cases. Put a scoop of ice cream on top with a cone for the clown's hat.

Make the features with fruit/sweets or squeezy sauces. (If the ice cream is coloured, mints with holes make good eyes, with half a mint for the mouth.)

PROGRAMME

Hello

The children stand in a circle. One child moves into the circle, stands facing the next child along, shakes his/her hand and says 'hello'. The second child answers 'hello' and the first one moves on round the circle to the next child, shaking hands and saying 'hello' again.

The second one follows the first round the circle – then the third and so on, until they are all following one another around.

The children stand in their original places when they reach them again. This game can go on for as long as you want it to.

Musical clown puppets

Props
2 clown finger puppets (See page 60 for instructions for making them)
Music

Sit the children in a circle. Whilst music is playing puppets have to be passed around. When it stops the two children holding them have to put them on and the 'clowns' have to 'perform': sing nursery rhymes, tell jokes, dance, say tongue twisters, etc. The two children can do it together or separately. Start music and pass the puppets around again.

Noise story: Noddy the clown

Adult to read the story and children to make the sound effects. Practise a few noises first. In particular, every time you say 'Noddy' tell them to nod their heads and clap twice. Decide what you will do for the other noises: wind ....., rain ..... and various circus animal noises ..... .

Living in the circus was a clown called Noddy ..... . One night, it was very stormy and he could hear thunder ..... . It was raining ..... and windy ..... and Noddy ..... became worried about the animals.
  He opened his caravan door ....., walked down three steps ..... and through the puddles ..... to their quarters.
  First he looked in at the lions ..... . They were fine and didn't seem worried at all. Next he visited the performing horses ....., then the elephants ....., and the seals ..... who were honking ..... and clapping their flippers ..... .
  There was another whistle of wind ..... and a clap of thunder ..... . Noddy ..... told them not to worry, because the storm ..... would soon be over.
  Just as he reached the chimps and monkeys ..... he heard a sound like Tarzan ..... . It was the circus Strong Man, who called

himself Tarzan .... Noddy ..... answered him with an Indian War Cry ....., just for fun. Together they looked in at the performing dogs ..... who were extremely pleased to see two friendly faces and barked with delight ....

The worst of the storm ..... was over now and it was quite quiet .... All was well and Noddy ..... and Tarzan ..... decided to go back to bed. They yawned ....., said 'Goodnight' to each other ....., and were soon in their beds and fast asleep ....

Ruby ring

Props
A ring

The children stand in a circle with their hands cupped and outstretched. In the middle of the circle stands the queen's servant, who has been entrusted with her ruby ring.

Holding it firmly in closed hands the servant goes through the motions of dropping the ring into the hands of the waiting children, saying to each one:

'My lady's lost her ruby ring,
Now tell me where to find it.'

Each child closes his/her hands and pretends to be holding the ring.

The servant secretly drops the ring into the hands of one of the children in the circle, and then touches another one on the shoulder and asks who has got the ring.

The one who has been touched by the queen's servant must then make a guess as to who has the ring. If (s)he is right, it is now his/her turn to be the servant. If (s)he is wrong (s)he has to bow three times and say 'sorry', and the servant touches another child until someone guesses correctly.

Toilet trip and wash hands ready to eat

*
Tea
*

Entertainment: An entertainer with 'circus' tricks, or a clown hand puppet. You could omit entertainment and go straight on to more games.

Chinese clown whispers

Sit children in a circle and whisper to one child – who whispers what she's heard to the next one, etc. When it gets to the last one he repeats it aloud! When you tell them what you started whispering, they will probably be surprised. Start with a different child next time or go round the opposite way. These three sentences will probably be enough:

Charlie Clown loved chocolate cakes.
A clown called Happy liked hopping.
My favourite clown tumbles down.

Action rhyme: Happy, the rocking clown

No matter how hard you try – he just won't stay down!
(*Children on knees throughout the rhyme.*)

I am Happy, the rocking clown.
   (*Smile and start to rock.*)
I am Happy, who never tumbles down.
   (*Continue rocking.*)
Side to side and to and fro,
   (*Sway sideways and then to and fro.*)
Always happy wherever I go.
   (*Laughing.*)

See what happens when I touch the ground.
   (*Touch floor as you fall over.*)
I pop back up because I am round.
   (*Pop back up.*)
Side to side and to and fro,
   (*Sway sideways and then to and fro.*)
Always happy wherever I go.
   (*Laugh as you continue swaying.*)

Pop goes the weasel

Props
Soft ball or bean bag

The children sit in a circle and pass round a soft ball while singing:

Half a pound of tuppenny rice,
Half a pound of treacle.
Mix it up and make it nice.
Pop goes the weasel.

On the word 'pop' the ball is thrown to a child on the opposite side of the circle, who has to try to catch it; the game and song start again.

Sing song

If you're happy and you know it clap your hands.
   (*Clap.*)
If you're happy and you know it clap your hands.
   (*Clap.*)
If you're happy and you know it then you're really going to show it.
If you're happy and you know it clap your hands.
   (*Clap.*)

Repeat verse, substituting the following actions:

Stamp your feet.
Nod your head.
Stand up straight.
Sit down quick.
Shout 'WE ARE'.

Take home

Clown finger puppet (as used in *Musical clowns*; instructions, page 60).

Yellow Party
(2 hours) *Indoors or outdoors*

Invitations

Materials
Thin yellow card
Envelopes (yellow if possible)
A yellow balloon for each invitation

Cut out a piece of card which when folded in half lengthwise will fit your envelope. Attach the balloon to the front and write 'A YELLOW PARTY' on it. Write your invitation inside (see Chapter 1 for suggested wording), and add, 'Please wear as much yellow as possible'.
   Make a few extra ones for thank you cards.

Decorations

Materials
Yellow balloons
Yellow paper/card
Cotton or string

Hang a bunch of yellow balloons on the door or the gate.

Indoors: Cut out yellow suns and moons, thread with cotton or string and suspend from ceiling.

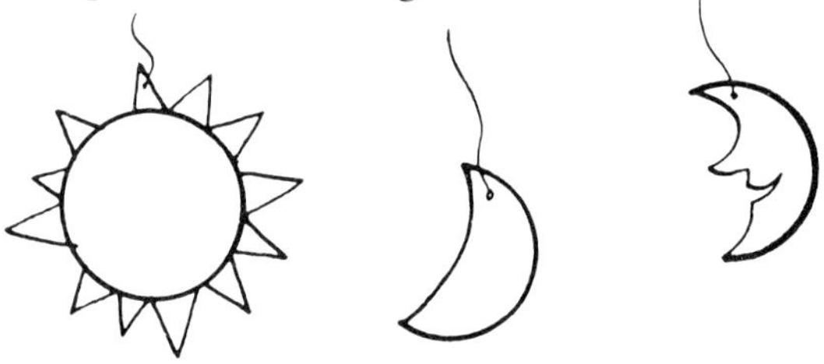

Outdoors: Hang yellow balloons and streamers from trees, poles, bushes, etc.

Name badges

Buy yellow stickers and write a child's name on each.

Place markers – indoors

Materials
Yellow card
Potatoes
Cocktail sticks
Silver foil

Cut card into sun or moon shapes, about 4–5 cm in diameter. Write the child's name on both sides. Blunt one end of a cocktail stick and split down a short way. Place the sun/moon in the split. Cover a small piece of potato (3–4 cm square) with silver foil and push the sharp end of the cocktail stick into it.

Cake

Make a round sponge and cover in yellow icing. Decorate with yellow sweets and yellow candles.

Food

Make yellow jellies and decorate food with yellow wherever possible. Serve yellow drinks. Have yellow tableware with a contrasting cloth (or the other way about if this is easier).

If the party is outside put the food in individual bags. Instead of place markers, use yellow sticky labels to match name badges, and attach them to the bags. Have a large rug or a blanket to sit on.

PROGRAMME

Woolly fun

Props
Yellow wool

Preparation before the party
Cut dozens of lengths of yellow wool – varying in length from about 3 to 15 centimetres.
Hide all the pieces of wool around the room or outdoor play area.

On the day
When the game starts tell everyone that they must search around for pieces of wool. The winner won't be the player with the most pieces of wool – but the one whose wool will make the longest line with the pieces end to end.

When all the wool has been found – or when no one can find any more – call the players together. Take the first player's 'find' and lay all the pieces end to end across the floor. Make a line with the second player's wool, parallel to the first, and starting, of course, in the same place. Do this with all the wool – and find the winner!

Giant's treasure

Props
Bell or tin full of small stones (or similar, so that it rattles)

It's better if an adult can start off being the Giant. He is blindfolded and stands a short way in front of the children. His treasure (the bell or tin) is placed a little way behind him.

The children line up and try to creep forward and take the treasure. The object is to get right up to it and ring the bell or shake the tin to prove you've done it. Any player who succeeds becomes the Giant.

If the Giant hears someone coming towards him he points in the direction of the sound, and if he's right the other player has to go back to the beginning. If he's wrong, though, the player can go on moving towards him.

Play the game until everyone has had a chance to try being as quiet as a mouse! And make sure that no one player is the Giant for long – everyone could take turns.

Oranges and lemons

Two adults (or two children) hold hands and form an arch, one side to be oranges and the other lemons. The other children, forming a chain, march underneath singing the song:

'Oranges and lemons,' say the bells of St Clement's.
'You owe me five farthings,' say the bells of St Martin's.
'When will you pay me?' say the bells of Old Bailey.
'When I grow rich,' say the bells of Shoreditch.
'When will that be?' say the bells of Stepney.
'I'm sure I don't know,' says the great bell of Bow.
Here comes a candle to light you to bed.
Here comes a chopper to chop off your head.

At the words 'chop off your head' the people in the 'arch' make a chopping movement up and down with their arms and catch one of the children passing underneath. The child caught is then asked to choose if (s)he wants to be an orange or lemon, but the other children must not hear his/her choice. (S)he then joins on behind the leader of the chosen side. When all the children have been caught like this and have joined one side or the other, the two teams have a tug-of-war.

Action rhyme: Wobbling yellow jellies

(*Children standing.*)

Wobble, wobble, wobble – what are we?
    (*All wobble – feet firm.*)
Wobbling yellow jellies for our tea.
    (*Continue.*)
Wobble, wobble, wobble from head to toes.
Wobble, wobble, wobble, even our nose.
    (*Twitch nose.*)
Wobble, wobble, wobble, – we can't stop.
Wobble, wobble, wobble – down we plop!
    (*All fall down.*)

Repeat, gradually getting faster and faster.

Toilet trip and wash hands ready for tea
*

Tea or picnic
*

Magic carpet

Props
Doormat
Whistle
Small prize

Put a small doormat on the floor (or on a piece of level ground) and let as many people as possible stand on this magic carpet. When the judge blows a whistle, everyone tries to push all the other passengers off the carpet and keep it for her/himself.

    Every few seconds the judge – who, of course, cannot see the carpet – blows the whistle, and those unlucky enough to have a foot off the carpet at that time are out.

    The game continues until only one person is left on the carpet. (S)he is declared the winner.

Fly away

The players stand facing you. They should each stand at least a metre apart, as this game can involve flailing arms!

Tell the players that you are going to call out the names of lots of animals and birds. Whenever you call out the name of a creature which can fly they must flap their arms. But sometimes you will call out the name of a creature which cannot fly – and woe betide any players caught flapping their arms then, they'll be out of the game! Let them go back in after missing a turn.

Players are out too if they do *not* flap their arms when you call out the name of a creature which can fly.

You can make this game lots of fun if you call out the names slowly at first, gradually getting faster.

Take home

A yellow balloon (from decorations) and/or a yellow lollipop.

Extra Games and Things to Do

Spoon and sweets race

Props
Small sweets
Paper cups
Spoons

Each player is given a spoon and a paper cup with his/her name on. Players must place their spoons and cups on the ground before them, as they stand in a line ready for the race to start.

Several metres away a number of sweets are sprinkled on the carpet or grass, and at the word GO the players must pick up their spoons, run over, with one hand behind their backs, pick up one sweet at a time with their spoons, run back and deposit the sweets in their paper cups.

The players must run backwards and forwards with the sweets until the whistle blows for the time limit. Any sweet dropping from the spoon must be returned to the sweet pile and picked up again.

Keep the sweets to take home.

Pass the clothes

Props
Old clothes (the funnier the better: hats, tops, trousers, bloomers, shoes, etc.)
Music

Sit the children in a circle and give them one item to pass around. Whoever is holding it when the music stops must put it on (and keep it on). Another item is then passed around, until the clothes run out. At the end, have a 'fashion parade'.

Creepy crawlies

Props
Team prize

This game is best played with no more than ten or twelve children. Split them into two teams. One team stands in a line side by side with legs wide apart and feet touching.

Members of the opposing team have to attempt to crawl from end to end of the line, weaving in and out through the spaces without *making a sound* or touching an opponent's leg.

If one of the standing team hears or feels anything, (s)he touches the crawler, who is then out of the game.

The winning team is the one whose players have most 'clear crawls'.

To make this game more difficult, blindfold the crawlers!

Ten green bottles

This is a game derived from the traditional song, with the children pretending to be bottles. If you have less, or only a few more, than ten guests, start singing with that number.

If you have larger numbers, put them in pairs (or even larger groups); each group equals one bottle!

Sing to the traditional tune:

Ten green bottles standing on the wall,
Ten green bottles standing on the wall,
If one green bottle should accidentally fall
    (*'Bottle' falls down.*)
There'll be nine green bottles standing on the wall.

Nine green bottles standing on the wall . . .

   (*Continue until all the bottles are lying in a heap.*)

Finger Puppets

Here are instructions for the clown finger puppet. You can use this pattern and change the trimmings to make other puppets.

Materials
Oddments of felt and other fabric
Wool and paper for decoration
Glue

Cut two pieces of felt the same length as your finger but 1 cm wider.

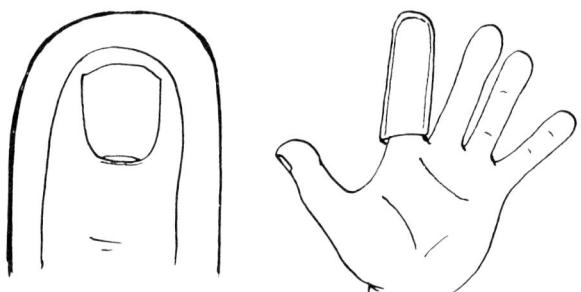

Glue the top and sides together, making a tube. Decorate as shown to make a clown with hat and ruffles.

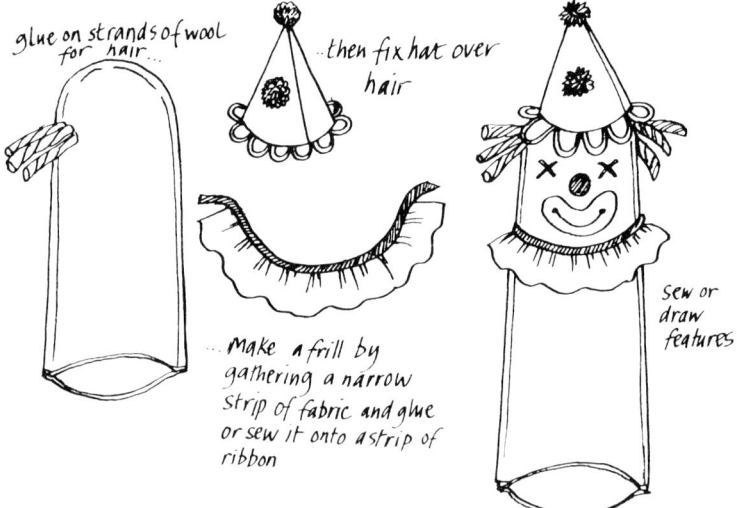

5
Parties for 7s and 8s

Balloon Party
(2½ hours) *Indoors*

Invitations

Materials
Thin card
Felt tips
String and glue
Envelopes

Cut the card into the shape of a balloon, as shown, to fit your envelopes. Attach a piece of string to it.

Write the invitation on the front and back. (See Chapter 1 for suggested wording.)

Make extra ones for thank you cards.

Decorations

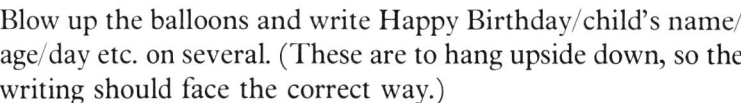

Materials
Balloons
Felt tips or pens which dry quickly

Blow up the balloons and write Happy Birthday/child's name/age/day etc. on several. (These are to hang upside down, so the writing should face the correct way.)

Blow up a balloon for each guest, and write a guest's name on each. If you have room, add the message, 'Thank you for coming to my party'. These will be for the guests to take home with them.

You can leave the going-home balloons blown up, or let them down again after you have labelled them. If you let them down, the children will have the fun of blowing them up to see what the message is.

Hang a bunch of balloons on the door.

Name badges

Materials
Round cardboard badges (from stationers)
Or stickers cut into the same shape as invitations
Glue, string and wool
Felt tip or pen

Write a name on each badge or sticker, and glue on a piece of string or wool to make it look like a balloon.

Place markers

Materials
Thin card
Felt tips

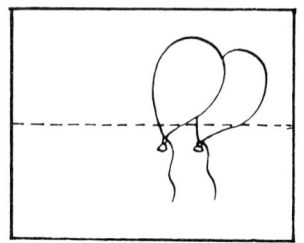

Cut out a piece of card 10 cm square. Mark a half-way line and draw some balloons as shown.

Write on the child's name. Cut around the balloons above the line. Fold in half so that the balloons stick up.

Cake – balloon

Bake a cake mixture in two pudding basins so that you have two roughly semicircular cakes. Marbled mixture (different colours swirled around) looks exciting when cut. Trim the tops level, place the cakes together (upright or sideways) and stick them together with fudge icing, before covering the whole circle with icing.

You can either paint on 'Happy Birthday' etc. with cake colouring, or swirl around the colours to match the inside. Add a brightly coloured ribbon or string to complete the balloon effect.

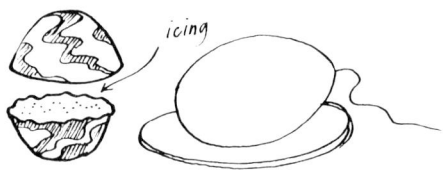

Food

Can be labelled with card balloons on cocktail sticks.

PROGRAMME

Party competition: Money box

(To be in progress throughout the party.)

Materials
Matchbox (or similar)
Sticky tape
An amount of money
A small cardboard box with a slit in the top (to post the answers)
Named piece of paper for each child
Pencil/pen

Put an amount of money in the matchbox and seal well with sticky tape. Tell the children it is more than 10p but less than 40p (or whatever you decide). During the party the children have to guess how much is inside, write it on their paper and post it. Open the postbox at the end of the party. The person who has guessed nearest to the amount wins the money.

Balloon battle

Props
One balloon

Children love this game, but a tough referee is needed to keep them seated! Arrange two rows of chairs facing each other for the children to sit on (alternatively, they could sit on the floor) with a no man's land between them. The two sides then do battle, hitting a balloon to and fro. The object is to hit it over the heads of their opponents: if it lands on the floor behind them a goal is scored. A whistle for 'half time' is an added refinement.

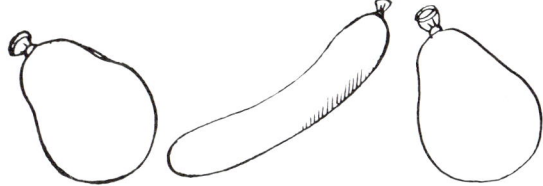

Second-hand shop

Props
Lots of old clothes
Cardboard box

This is a hilarious, chaotic game that everyone enjoys playing. Gather together a good pile of old clothes, all shapes and sizes, even small items of clothing like gloves and socks, the funnier the better.

At the start of the game put one article less than the number of children into the box. (You will need to add more each time as the children still in the game keep on the clothes.)

The children line up at the other end of the room and on the word go they all run up to the box, pick up a garment and put it on. The one left without a garment can help you next time. Continue putting clothes in the box, one less each time, until you have a winner with lots of clothes on!

Don't drop a balloon

Props
Lots of blown-up balloons with no strings hanging (keep well hidden until now)
List of questions
Prize

This is a lively game and all you'll need are lots and lots of big balloons. Ask the players to stand in line, facing you. You, as question-master, go to the first player and ask him or her a question.

If (s)he answers correctly you move on to player number two and ask him or her a question. If (s)he answers correctly pass on to the next player and so on.

If, however, one of the players answers incorrectly, (s)he is given two large balloons (without strings) to hold. Carry on asking questions that are more and more difficult, and you'll find that the players have more and more balloons to hold on to. In fact, when their arms are full and they have a balloon between their knees, you'll find that they'll probably begin to drop them. Any player who drops a balloon is out, and the last player left in is the winner.

(The winner might be holding many balloons successfully, or be a clever clogs who has answered all the questions right and so has no balloons to carry.)

Keep the balloons for the last game.

Musical pillows

Props
Pillow or cushion
Music
Prize

Sit the children on the floor in a circle, each one quite far from the other. Get them to throw a pillow to each other when the music is playing. When the music stops the child holding the pillow is out. Not very easy when you are sitting down!

Rocket race

Props
Balloon for each child
Prize

Here's a chance for everyone to send up their own rocket into space! Each competitor is given a balloon of a different colour (or marked differently) which they must blow up and hold tightly so that the air will not escape.

They then line up at the starting point, and at the word GO everyone lets go and allows their balloon to soar high in the air.

The 'rockets' will travel until all the air is released; and then they will fall to the ground. The one which has travelled the farthest is the winner.

Sweet bashing

Props
One or two strong carrier bags
Sweets
Wooden spoon/spatula/ruler (or similar)
Cup hook
String

Put a selection of small sweets in a tough carrier bag (or put one bag inside another to make the game last longer). Tie firmly at the top and, using string, suspend the bag from a cup hook fixed in a doorway. Line the children up and give them each a turn at whacking the bag with a wooden spoon or similar. Eventually the bag bursts and they all scramble for the sweets.

Toilet trip and wash hands ready to eat
*
Tea
*

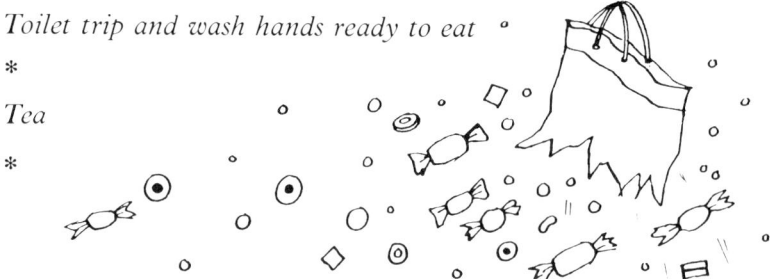

Noise story: The balloon shop

Props
Cassette or tape recorder

Explain to the children that you're going to record a story for radio and that as you have no sound effects, they will have to make them. Tell them also that they will be able to hear the result. Practise a few, i.e. every time you say 'balloon' they have to shout 'POP' and clap hands; 'blow' . . . they blow; 'Mr Bell' . . . ting-a-ling; 'feeling ill' . . . loud coughs, or groans.
   Switch the cassette/tape recorder to record and start reading:

The man who owned the balloon ..... shop was called Mr Bell ..... . In his shop he sold lots of different balloons ..... . People always wanted to test them, so quite often they blew ..... and blew ..... and blew ..... until the balloon burst ..... . This made Mr Bell ..... very nervous and he never knew whether to laugh ..... or cry ..... . Sometimes it gave him hiccups ..... .

One particular day Mr Bell ..... was feeling ill ..... and he hoped no one would blow ..... up a balloon ..... until it burst ..... .

The door opened ..... and Mrs Gunn ..... came in accompanied by a bee ..... . It flew all around Mr Bell's ..... head; it buzzed ..... all around. Down it buzzed ..... , up it buzzed ..... , and landed on his nose. Mr Bell ..... shouted ..... then sneezed ..... . Mrs Gunn ..... was so confused she left the shop, followed by the bee ..... .

Mr Bell ..... decided he was feeling too ill ..... to keep open his shop which sold balloons ..... .

All the way to his bed he yawned ..... and sneezed ..... and yawned ..... . But at last he fell fast asleep ..... .

Play back the recording.

Burst the balloon
(Very noisy!)

Props
Blown-up balloon for each child (no strings)
Whistle
Prize

Let the children choose a balloon each. Get them to stand well spread out around the room and tell them to hold the balloons over their heads for the 'start whistle'. The object of this extremely noisy and boisterous game is for them to burst each other's balloons, whilst trying to retain their own (in any way they can). Stop the game with the whistle when you see just one balloon left – the winner!

Competition answer

Ready for a rest now, so open the 'answer box' and read the guesses out. Open the matchbox and count out the money. Give it to the person who has the nearest answer.

Take home

A balloon with a message. (See *Decorations* at beginning of this chapter.)

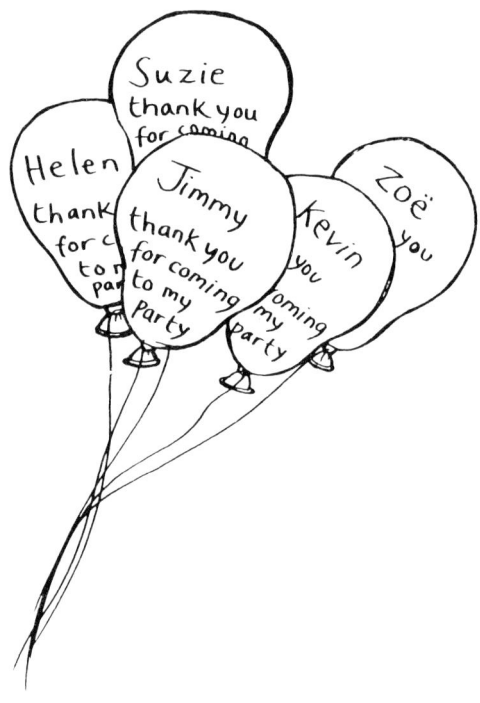

Animal Party
(2½ hours) *Indoors or outdoors*

Invitations

Materials
Paper (fairly stiff)
Felt tips
Envelopes

Cut out the paper, so that when folded it will fit inside your envelope. Draw a snake on the outside, as shown, and write, 'To make me come alive, colour me and cut along the dotted lines'.

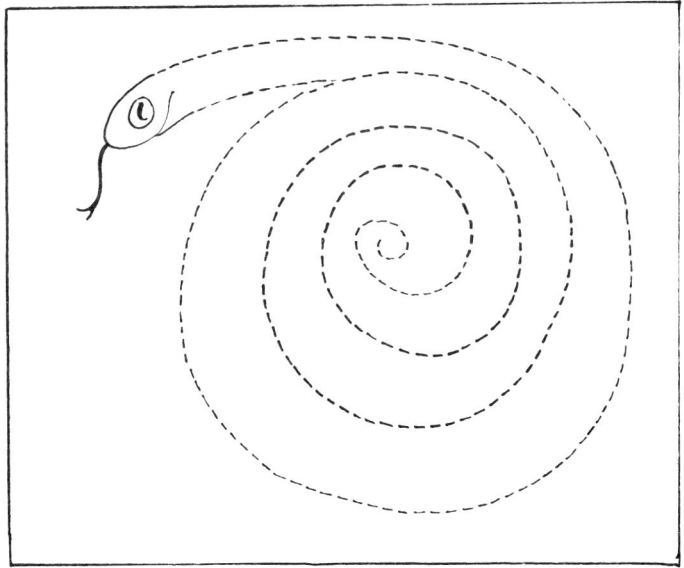

Write the invitation to the party on the inside. (See Chapter 1 for suggested wording.)
Make extras for thank you cards.

Decorations

Materials
Paper plates
Animal pictures cut out from magazines etc.
Glue
String or cord

Glue the animal pictures on to both sides of the plates. Make one hole and thread the string through.
   Suspend from ceiling (or trees/bushes if outside).

Materials
Animal poster or large cut-out animal

Attach to front door or garden gate.

Name badges

Materials
Large round blank stickers
Felt tips

Draw the outline of an animal's face on the sticker, as shown.

   Write the child's name on it and cut out.

Place markers – animal masks

Materials
Thin card – assorted colours
Paint/pens
Thin elastic

Draw an animal mask, as shown. Colour and cut out. Thread elastic through both sides, as shown, and write the child's name on the inside of the mask.

Put a mask at each child's place with the name facing towards the child. Let the children wear the masks during tea.

Or, if you're having a picnic, hand them out with the food.

Cake – caterpillar

Make or buy two small Swiss rolls or one large one.

Cover with green icing; use Matchmakers or chocolate fingers for legs and small round sweets for features.

Use food colour to paint the icing in stripes, so that it looks like a caterpillar's striped body.

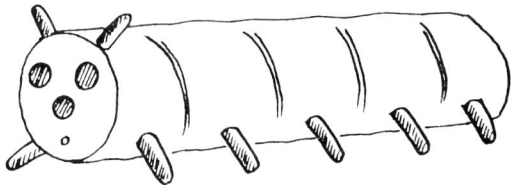

Food

Indoors
Use animal shape cutters as much as possible for biscuits and sandwiches. Make small Swiss rolls into baby caterpillars, using sweets for features and legs as you did for the cake. Make a sausage hedgehog by cutting a large potato into a rough hedgehog shape and sticking small sausages all over it (impaled on cocktail sticks). Put the hedgehog on a bed of lettuce.

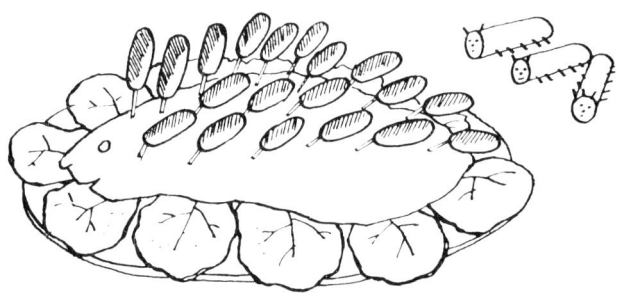

Outdoors: animals' picnic
Place a 'food parcel' and named mask for each child in a circle, ready for them to find.

If the ground is damp, straw bales are ideal for sitting on (obtainable from pet shops). Alternatively you could cut out individual plastic mats from bin bags.

PROGRAMME
Party competition: What's inside?

Materials
Two toy animals (one soft toy and one plastic)
Soft wrapping paper and a piece of polythene or fabric
String or sticky tape
Piece of paper and pencil (for yourself)

Before the party
Wrap up the animals in separate parcels, so that the children can feel through. Use layers of soft wrapping paper first, then add an outer wrapping of polythene or fabric. This will stop the children poking their fingers inside. Secure the parcels well and if possible hang them up. It's far more difficult to 'feel' a suspended parcel!

On the day
Number the parcels and tell the children that during the party they have to guess what's inside.

When they have made up their minds, they should whisper the answer to you. Record their answers on your sheet of paper.

At the end you will open the parcels and give a prize to the winner. (Or use the contents as the prize.)

Animal team game

Props
Paper cut into small squares
Wool (several different colours)
Felt tip
Whistles
Team prize

Before the party
The children will be divided into teams of equal numbers, each bearing an animal's name. Decide how many teams you want (depending on the number of guests you have), then choose the team names e.g. cow, cat, dog, horse, rooster, duck. On each slip of paper write a team animal's name, one slip for each team member, so that you have an equal number for each animal. Fold the slips of paper and put them in a hat or box.

Shortly before the party starts you will need to prepare the wool. You will need a different colour for each team, and an equal length of each colour (about a metre of each). Cut the wool into unequal pieces but nothing less than 5 cm, and place it all round the room (on chair legs, over door handles, along skirting boards, etc.) or outside on bushes, window ledges etc., all round the garden.

On the day
Ask the children to take a slip of paper from the bag, keeping it folded. At the blow of the whistle they have to unfold their paper and make the noise of the animal whose name they find on it. They listen for people making the same noise and link up with them. When the teams are complete, ask each one to choose a leader.

Each team has to collect a different coloured wool. The members of the team hunt for the wool but they are not allowed to touch it. When they see a piece of wool they stand in front of it and make the noise of their team animal. The leader then comes along and picks up the piece of wool.

After ten minutes, they join all the collected pieces of wool together, and the team with the longest string is the winner.

Bunny hops

Before you start this game, it might be a good idea to let everyone practise doing some bunny hops, or springs, around the garden or across the floor. First of all choose three 'ferrets', the rest of the players are then called 'bunnies'. At the starting signal the bunnies leave the corners of the garden or room which are their burrows, and hop and spring around, while the ferrets lie in wait in the middle. When the signal 'Go ferrets' is given they rush around on all fours, trying to catch as many bunnies as they can before they reach the safety of their burrows. The last bunny in is the winner.

Dead lions
(*A quiet game.*)

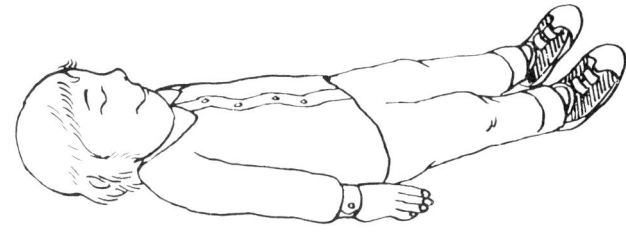

Props
Music
Prize

The children jump up and down to music and when it stops they must lie down on the floor and pretend to be dead lions. Anyone who laughs or moves is out – and you have to try and get them out. You must not touch them, but must try to make them laugh or move by verbal means only. 'There's a spider on your arm,' etc. As soon as someone is out, he/she must get up and help you try to get the others out. The person who stays still longest wins.

Lap it up

Props
Dice and cup
Mittens (for extra effect make a 'tail' as well)
Squash in a plastic saucer
Spare squash to replenish it

Sit the children in a circle with the saucer of squash in the middle. Let the children take it in turns to throw a dice. Anyone who throws a six has to put on the mittens, crawl to the saucer and lap it up. When someone else throws a six they have to change places with the 'cat'.

Toilet trip and wash hands (and faces)

*

Tea or picnic

*

Noise story: Polly Parrot and Cyril

Props
Cassette or tape recorder

Explain to the children that you're going to record a story for radio and that as you have no sound effects they will have to make them. Tell them also that they will be able to hear the result. Practise a few, e.g. every time you say 'Mr Duck' they have to shout 'quack, quack'; when you say 'lion' – roar; 'Polly Parrot' – 'Hello, Pretty Polly, Pretty Polly'.

Switch the tape recorder to 'record' and start reading:

Once upon a time there was a zookeeper called Mr Duck ..... . He was extremely proud of his zoo, in particular the lions ..... and the laughing hyenas ..... but the one thing he couldn't stand was Polly the Parrot ..... . Every time she saw Mr Duck ..... she would say ..... . Not just when she saw Mr Duck ..... , but whenever she met any of the visitors she would say ..... .

In the children's corner there lived a rooster ..... and he was the only one who could frighten Polly Parrot ..... . When he strutted about crowing ..... you couldn't hear Polly Parrot ..... . Mr Duck ..... wished he could train him to crow ..... all day, but that was impossible.

One day when Mr Duck ..... was looking at the lions ..... and the laughing hyenas ..... he had an idea, just as Polly Parrot ..... flew by. He would get another parrot and train it to shout back at her. He found a parrot called Cyril and taught him to shout 'Shut up' whenever he saw another parrot.

Here you switch the tape recorder off and tell the children that when you come to Cyril in the story they must shout 'shut up'. Start to record again.

Mr Duck ..... put Cyril ..... on his shoulder to do his rounds. Of course, quite soon who should fly by but Polly Parrot ..... . Cyril shouted back ..... . Polly Parrot ..... was extremely surprised to hear Cyril ..... .

She couldn't believe it, so once more Polly said ..... , and once more Cyril replied ..... . Polly was so cross that she flew to the top of the nearest tree. In fact, she stayed there all day. This made Mr Duck ..... very pleased and he laughed ..... as loud as his laughing hyenas ..... and was immediately told off by Cyril ..... .

Say, 'All right, I will', and stop! Play back the recording.

Animal talk

Props
Blindfold

Get the children to kneel in a circle facing inwards, with one child in the middle, blindfolded. (S)he has to crawl towards the edge of the circle (feeling where (s)he is by touching only the other children's knees), and choose one person, to whom (s)he says, 'Speak, dog, speak' (or cat, donkey, rooster, etc.). The person chosen has to make the animal noise requested.

If the person in the blindfold can name the person making the noise, they exchange places, otherwise (s)he chooses again. When a new player is blindfolded the children can move to new positions in the circle if they want to.

Danger zone (or Cow pat!)

Props
Circle of brown wrapping paper
Prize

The players form a circle and hold hands. In the middle is the cow pat – it is the danger zone.

The circle begins to move round. As it goes, the players bump against each other and each makes an effort to push his/her neighbour on to the cow pat. The slightest touch of a foot on the paper means the victim is out. The ring reforms minus the victim, and proceeds. The last in is the winner.

Old MacDonald

A loud rendition of this traditional song is always great fun.

Old MacDonald had a farm
E-i-e-i-o,
And on that farm he had a duck
E-i-e-i-o,
With a quack, quack here,
And a quack, quack there,
Here a quack – there a quack –
Everywhere a quack, quack.
Old MacDonald had a farm
E-i-e-i-o.

Continue with different animals.

Competition answer

First read out what the children thought was in the parcels. Unwrap the parcels. Either give the winner what is inside or have a small prize ready. If no one has guessed correctly, you could give a prize for the nearest try.

Take home

Animal masks and/or an animal-shaped chocolate bar or animal finger puppet.

Extra Games and Things to Do

Blow the feather

Props
Tablecloth
Feather (small)

All the children, except one, hold the cloth tightly. Place the feather in the middle of the cloth, which the lone child has to try to grab. At the same time, the others have to blow it away.

Run for the tumbler

Props
One tough plastic tumbler
Team prize

Here's an energetic outdoor game for three or more teams of equal numbers. Starting with one, each member of the team is given a number. If there are three teams there will be three players with the number 'one', three players with the number 'two', and so on.

Starting with Team A in numerical order, then team B in numerical order, the teams sit down in a wide circle, equally spaced, and the unbreakable tumbler is placed in the centre of the circle. It is best if you have a judge for this game, who can act as starter.

The starter calls out a number and the players who have that number leap up and run round the circle in a clockwise direction. When they reach their own place in the circle they dive into the centre and grab the tumbler. The first player to reach the tumbler gains a point for his/her team, and the team with the most points after all the numbers have been called is the winner.

Flour mountain

Props
Flour
Jelly sweet
Teaspoon

Make a mountain out of flour (mould it in a pudding basin and tip it out). Place a jelly sweet centre top. Using the teaspoon each child has to take out a spoonful of flour. The one who causes the sweet to move can eat it – by picking it out of the flour with his/her mouth!

Pick a pea (or bean)

Props
Dried peas (or beans)
Container and straw for each child
Prize

A pile of dried peas (or beans) is set in the centre of the room.

A small container is set beside each child and each player is given a straw.

The game is to see which person can transport the most peas, breath held, from the pile to the container. The player with the greatest number of peas (or beans) at the end of a given time is the winner. *Safety note:* Do not use red kidney beans, which are dangerous to eat when uncooked.

Try a tongue twister

Practise these once all together, then get the children to take turns at saying each one. You could give a prize to the person who says each one clearest and fastest.

Tom taught Tim to throw three times.
Ben bought Bet blue and black buttons.
Betty bought a beautiful bat and ball for Bob's birthday.

6
Parties for 9s and 10s

Card Party
(2½–3 hours) *Indoors*

Invitations – playing cards

Materials
Thin white card
Felt tips/paints
Envelopes

Cut out a piece of card to fit your envelope. Decorate one side to look like a playing card (nines or tens according to birthday being celebrated), and write the invitation on the reverse side (see Chapter 1 for suggested wording). Make extras for thank you cards.

Decorations – cards and suits

Materials
Thin card: white, black and red
String/cord
Felt tips/paints

Using white card, cut out large oblong shapes and decorate as playing cards.

From black and red card cut hearts, diamonds, clubs and spades. Make one hole at the top of each.

Thread string/cord through the hole and suspend from the ceiling or hang around the room.

Make a large playing card for the front door.

Name badges

If all the children know each other, these may not be necessary.

Materials
Red and black card
Safety pins
Sticky tape
White pencil or silver/gold metallic felt tip

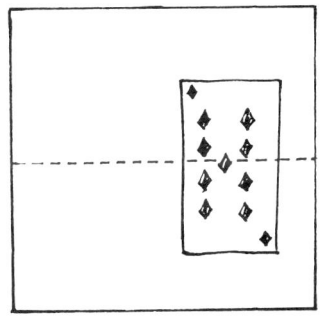

Cut out heart, diamond, spade and club shapes and attach a safety pin to the back of each, using pieces of sticky tape. Write on each, 'Hi! I'm ..... '.

Place markers

Materials
White card
Felt tips/paint

Cut out a piece of card 10 cm square. Mark a half-way line and draw a playing card as shown.

Cut around the card above the half-way line, fold in half and write on the child's name.

Special equipment

If you do all the games in this section, you will need at least five packs of cards (more if you are having a very large party), so that you can prepare the games in advance. It is not possible to get by with just one pack. So be prepared to borrow from friends.

Cake – card

Bake or buy an oblong cake. Ice it in a playing card design. Use white icing and either paint (with food colours) or pipe on the 9 or 10 (according to which birthday is being celebrated) of whichever suit the birthday person prefers.

Food

Using four suits (spades, diamonds, hearts, clubs), make labels for the food out of thin card. If you blunt one end of a cocktail stick and split it slightly, the card will slide into the split.

Make biscuits in diamond, club, etc., shapes and ice them appropriately.

PROGRAMME
Party competition: Eight eights

Props
A small note pad and pencils
Postcard

Write clearly on the postcard:

   WRITE DOWN EIGHT EIGHTS SO THAT THEY ADD UP TO 1000

Pin the postcard up, and show it to the children when they arrive. Tell them the competition will last throughout the party or until someone has solved it. The paper and pencils will be available for them to work on the problem, between games.

What card am I?

Props
Paper or pack of cards
Felt tips
Safety pins

Make up imitation cards (or use real ones). Pin one on the back of each child.

Note: Make sure you pin on an equal number of each suit, as you are also making up teams for the next game. If you have a number of guests which is not divisible by four, enlist your helpers to make up one team. If this is not possible, omit one suit (if your total number of players divides by three but not four) or two suits (if your total number divides by two but not four).

When everyone has a card on their back, they have to find out what it is by asking questions of each other. But – the answers are limited to 'yes' or 'no'. Everyone has to find out what they are and join up with those of the same suit.

Hunt the cards
(Very noisy!)

Props
Pack of cards

Use a suit for each team in the game and hide them about the room (face down).

Ask each team to choose a leader. Tell each leader which suit the team must find. At the 'off' the members of each team have to hunt for the cards of their suit, but only the team leader is allowed to turn them over.

When they find a card, they must stand in front of it and shout, 'Heart, Heart' (or whatever) and the leader must come and examine it. They must not shout out anything else except the name of their suit. The first team to find their complete suit is the winner.

Throwing cards

Props

Playing cards (you may need more than one pack, depending on the size of your party)
Basket or box
Prize

Place the basket or box a reasonable distance away from a marked line. Give the children five or six cards each, to try to throw into the basket in turns.

Grab the Joker

Props
Joker
Score card
Team prize

Divide the children into teams of equal numbers. Number each child in the team 1 – 2 – 3, etc., so that each team is identically numbered. If there are four teams, for example, there will be four number ones, four number twos, etc.

Keeping team members together in numerical order, ask the children to sit in one large circle. Place the Joker in the middle.

You call out a number, and all the players who have that number must leap up, and run round the outside of the circle in a clockwise direction. For example, if you call 'Number three' the threes have to run. When they reach their own place in the circle, they must dive into the centre and grab the Joker. The first player to reach it gets a point for her/his team, and the team with the most points after all the numbers have been called is the winner.

Tidy up for tea

*

Tea

*

Entertainment: Card tricks.

If you know someone who can do a few card tricks, this would make ideal entertainment. Alternatively, you could ask beforehand if any of the guests (or the party person) would like to show the others a trick or two.

Find the ace

Props
An ace card (a small one if possible)

Hide the ace in quite a difficult place, but so that it can be seen without moving anything. The children start to search and when they have spotted it, come and whisper where it is to you. If they are right they have to sit down in the middle of the room. The whole search must be done in silence, although much giggling will take place. The last one to find it has to do a forfeit. (A good forfeit: stand with your back against the wall, heels touching the skirting board, and pick up an ace card from the floor, placed about 30 cm in front. Heels and feet must not be moved.)

Swop shop

Props
Coloured card
A bag for each child
Whistle
Prize

Before the party
Cut out lots of circles about 2 cm in diameter from different coloured card. Draw a heart or club or spade or diamond on to each circle (one for each circle).

Make up sets of three (three hearts, etc.), enough for at least two sets of three for each guest.

On the day
Spread the circles over the floor and on the furniture. Give each child a bag to put them in.

When the whistle blows the players have to collect as many circles as they can. When no more can be found tell them that the object of the game is to get as many matching sets of three as possible.

Give them time to sort their circles into sets. They can lay down completed sets, and keep the remaining ones available for swopping. To get the swops going, form the children into a circle. Explain to them that they must decide how many they are going to swop at a time (remembering that the winner is the one with most sets).

When the whistle blows, they must hold up their hands (being careful that no one can see what is on the circles) and call out the number of circles they want to swop. The swops are made 'blind', that is, no one knows what they are getting when they make a swop.

Players can swop only with someone who has the same number to swop. Carry on swopping until all the discs have been used up. The person with most sets of three is the winner and receives a small prize.

Tied up in knots

Props
Pack of cards
String

Before the party
Sort the cards so that they are in pairs – two red 3s, two black 4s, two red queens, etc. You will need one card for each child (the rest of the pack will not be needed). Equal numbers of people are essential for this game, so you might have to make up the numbers yourself or with a helper.

On the day
Deal out the sorted cards, one to each child, and tell them that they have to find the person who holds the other half of their pair, who will be their partner.

When they have found their partners, stand them in pairs facing each other. Give each person a piece of string (about 30 cm long) to hold in his/her right hand. The left hand must be down by his/her side.

Using right hands only, each pair has to tie their string together, with three or four knots – depending on how difficult you want it to be. You can bet there'll be a few people tied up in knots by the end of this game!

Competition answer

Ask if anyone has found the correct way to make eight eights add up to 1000 and if they have, to prove it!

If no one has come up with the answer – show them:

```
 888
  88
   8
   8
   8
————
1000
————
```

Take home

A miniature pack of cards.

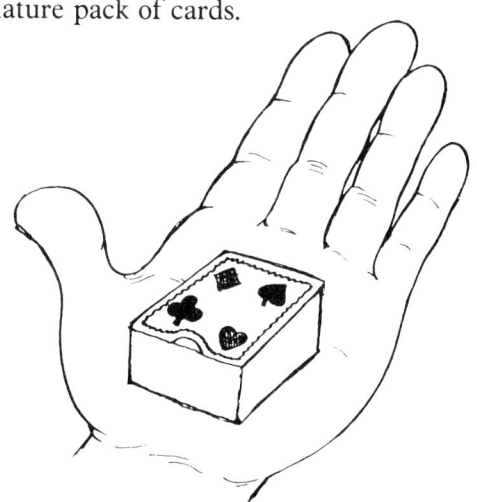

Sports party
(2½–3 hours) *Outdoors*

Invitations – admission ticket

Materials
Thin card
Felt tips
Envelopes

Cut the cards to fit your envelopes and word the invitation to read like an admission ticket to a match/sports event. (See the picture below for suggested wording.)
Make extra for thank you cards.

> **GRAND SPORTS PARTY**
> THURSDAY 18TH JULY
> VENUE: 10 ACACIA AVENUE
> KICK OFF: 3·00PM
> MATCH ENDS: 6·00 PM
>
> In honour of 's birthday, a grand trophy will be presented to the winner, with valuable certificates for runners up.

Decorations – banners

Materials
Old sheets or plain tablecloths
Marker pens
String

Cut the material into different sized oblong strips and attach a piece of string to each corner.

On each banner write a message or 'event' e.g. 'Happy Birthday', 'Pancake race', 'Arsenal v. Manchester United', '100 metres hurdles', etc. and the date. Make one for the entrance which says 'Welcome'.

Name badges

May not be necessary for children of this age, but you could give them all 'competitor' numbers and use these instead of names during the party.

Attach the numbers to the back and front of each competitor, using string or sticky tape.

Place markers

You should not need these. As the party will be outside, it's a good idea to have a picnic or barbecue, with informal seating arrangements.

Cake – games pitch

Decorate the cake to resemble the pitch of a favourite sport, for example, football, rugby, cricket, hockey, netball, tennis. Use green icing as a base and pipe on white icing for 'line' markings (or paint on brown/black lines with cake colouring). Use plastic toy models for the players.

Food

You could have 'food parcels', *or* bangers and beans, *or* bangers and mash, all eaten outside with fresh fruit and birthday cake to finish.

Or you could have a barbecue: sausages, burgers and/or chicken drumsticks, accompanied by rolls, sauces and salad, and followed by the cake.

Special equipment

In the programme that follows, you will need to divide your competitors into groups of various sizes, depending on the game. To choose the teams or groups, use coloured discs drawn from a hat or box by the competitors. You will need to make enough different coloured discs to divide your guests into two teams, or into groups of three or four, according to the rules of the game.

Work out how many discs you will need for the number of guests you are inviting, and make extra in each colour to keep handy in case some get lost.

Materials for the discs
Stiff card in several colours
Scissors

You will also need
Starting and finishing lines (use thick tape weighted down with stones)
Whistle
Stopwatch – useful if you can get hold of one

Trophies and scores

Buy a trophy for the overall winner and certificates for all the others. Alternatively, have trophies for 1st, 2nd and 3rd and then certificates.

Award points for placings and mark them on a 'scoreboard' (blackboard or similar) after each game. Your points system could go like this:

Individual games	Winner gets 3 points
Winning groups	3 points for each player
Winning teams	3 points for each player

(If there are 2nds, score 2; 3rds, score 1.)

PROGRAMME

Party competition: Name that face

Props
Cut-outs of well-known sports personalities (numbered)
Paper plates (or similarly sized pieces of card)
Glue
String
Postcard for each person
Pencil for each person

Glue the pictures of sports personalities on both sides of the plates or cardboard (a different one on each side). Make a hole in the top of each plate or cardboard disc and thread the string through. Suspend from branches, bushes, etc. Give each person a postcard and pencil and explain that this game is to last throughout the party so there's plenty of time to recognize the personalities. They must hand in their completed postcards just before the end of the party.

Balloon race (individual)

Props
Balloon for each competitor
String or thread for ties

Arrange a pile of deflated balloons at one end of the garden and some pieces of string or thread to use as ties when they are blown up.
   When you blow the whistle, the children run to the balloons, blow them up, tie them and head them back to the starting point. Whoever reaches it first is the winner.

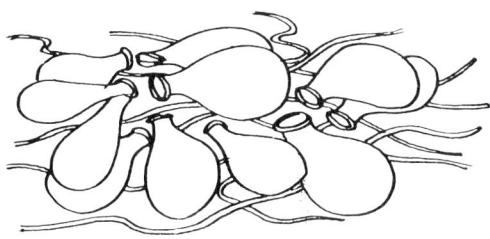

Pancake race (teams)

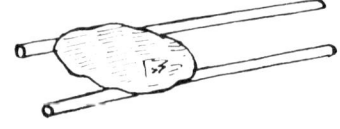

Props
Newspaper 'pancakes' (about 10 cm in diameter) – one for each competitor
Pieces of dowel (or similar) about 20 cm long (the 'pan'). You will need two pieces for each team.
Paper plate for each team

Place the pancakes flat on the ground at the far end of the garden. Give the first member of each team the 'frying pan' and put the plate at his/her feet.

At the word 'go' the first member of each team must run and pick up a pancake and, keeping it *flat* on the top of the 'pan', get it back down the garden and put it on the plate. This has to be done very carefully as any quick or jerky movement causes the pancake to topple. If the pancake falls, it must be returned to the end of the garden and picked up again.

Continue until each team member has put a pancake on the plate. First team to do so wins the game.

Four-legged race (groups of 3)

Props
Ties for legs

The players stand next to each other in threes. The legs of the competitor in the centre are tied to those of his/her teammates, making 'four legs' (see diagram).

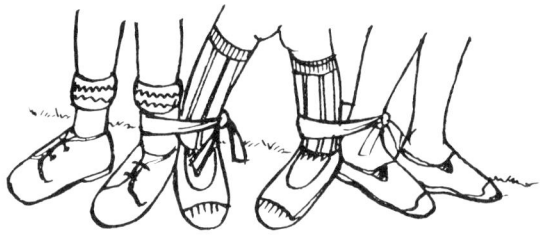

The threes line up at the starting line and, at the whistle, race to the finishing line and back again. Much of the fun comes at the turn.

One important rule: the race has to be run *in silence*. Noisy threes are sent back to the starting line!

If you have a stopwatch, you can allow the threes to race one at a time against the clock. This way is probably more entertaining and easier to judge.

Handicap football (teams)

Props
Large wellies or shoes (much too big for the competitors)
Small ball (tennis or similar)
Markers for goal areas

This can be either one game or played in heats. It will depend on the number of competitors, the size of your 'pitch' and the number of *large* shoes or wellies you can find.

Give a time limit to the whole game. Longer if only one game and shorter if there are heats.

Each player has to wear a pair of shoes or wellies (these are best). Use a small ball and forget all the usual rules of football. Place the ball in the middle of the pitch; blow the whistle; stand clear and let them score goals.

*

Tidy up for tea, picnic or barbecue

*

Entertainment: Acrobatic stunts.
Before the party, you could ask each guest (or groups of guests) to come prepared to perform their own athletic feats, stunts or tricks – juggling, for example.

Tortoise race (individual)

Line up the competitors on all fours. Mark out a finishing line. Blow the whistle and off they go as slowly as possible. The last one home is the winner – but *they have to keep moving* or they will be eliminated.

Cock fighting (pairs)

A boisterous game for two contestants at a time.

Props
Two large handkerchiefs (or pieces of fabric) to tie ankles together
Two walking sticks or similar

Sit the two contestants on the ground facing each other. Ask them to lift their knees up and grasp them. Now tie each one's ankles together. Push a walking stick (or similar) under their knees, but over their arms. They must now wriggle towards each other until their toes touch. At the word 'Go' they must try to capsize each other – using only their feet.

Buckets game (groups of 4)

Props
Empty washing-up-liquid bottles (one bottle for each team)
Bucket or container for each team
One extra bucket

Mark a starting and a finishing line, and arrange all the buckets but one along the finishing line. The groups line up along the starting line, the first player in each group holding a plastic bottle.

The extra bucket has to be full of water, and you'll also have to have a means of topping it up now and then. Put this bucket behind the finishing line, where it can be reached easily by all the groups.

The first player in each group waits for the whistle and then races over to the water bucket. (S)he gets as much water as possible into the plastic bottle – without taking the nozzle off – and then races across the course to the group's bucket on the finishing line. There (s)he squirts all the water into that bucket, before racing back to give the bottle to the next player in the group.

The game goes on for some minutes, or until everyone has had a turn – and then the winners are judged. The winning group is the one with the most water in its bucket on the finishing line.

Competition answers

Read out the correct solutions. Check the results. Award three points to the person with most correct guesses, two points to the second, one to the third.

Final scores

Presentation of trophies and certificates.

Extra Games and Things to Do

Treasure Hunt (pairs)

Props
String cut into 30–40 cm pieces, one piece for each two competitors

Fold the pieces of string in half and hold the folded end of all the pieces in your hand. Let the competitors hold a loose end each. Release the string and pairs will be holding either end of one piece of string!

Props
Paper bag for each pair
List of objects to find
Two prizes (or add points to total)

Give each pair a bag to put their treasures in. Make and pin up a list of 'Treasure Trove' for them to collect. Ideas for treasure will vary according to the location, but here are a few suggestions: hanky, coloured shoe, 2p, stone, feather, sock, necklace, ring, leaves of various kinds, twigs. Hide some items under things, on things, etc.

The first pair to collect all the items on your list wins the game.

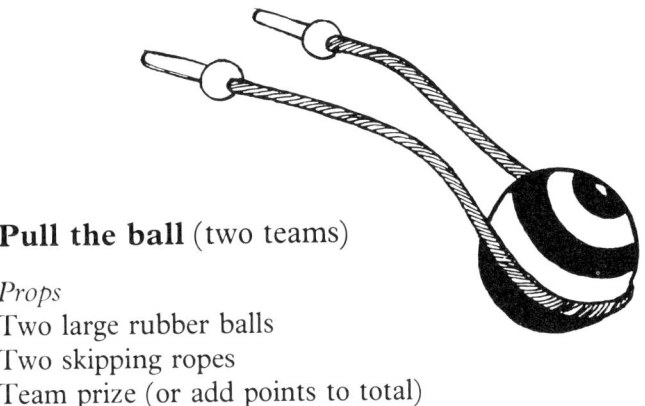

Pull the ball (two teams)

Props
Two large rubber balls
Two skipping ropes
Team prize (or add points to total)

Divide into teams. Place a chair at the far end of the garden/room. Beginning at a starting line, each member of the team has to make a loop around the ball with the string, and then pull the ball backwards up to the chair, around it and back to the starting line. When each person returns the next one has to go. Harder than it sounds.

Animal pairs (two teams)

Props
Prepared cards
Safety pins
Team prize (or add points to total)

Write the names of well-known animals on cards and cut the cards in half (for example, li - on, rab - bit, ho - rse). Divide the children into two teams and pin one half of a card on the back of each child. Make sure the matching pairs are in the same team (to make this easy use different coloured cards for each team). The children are allowed only to ask each other questions like 'Do I have spots?' 'What colour am I?' – that is, questions about the characteristics of the animal. The first team to find all their pairs wins the game.

Stepping stones (individual)

Props
3 pieces of newspaper for each player (about 25 cm square)
Prize (or add points to total)

Mark out a course in your garden/room with a finishing line and a starting line about three metres apart.

Give each player three squares of paper. These are to be used as stepping stones, and (s)he must get across the course, stepping only on them – moving them along as (s)he goes.

Any player stepping on the ground is disqualified and the first to reach the finishing line wins.

Jump the stick (individual)

Props
A stick about 45 cm long for each player
No prizes or points – just fun

Anyone can jump over a stick only 30–60 cm (a foot or two) above the ground – or can they?

Take a stick about 45 cm long and hold it in front of you, one hand at each end of the stick and bending your back so that the stick is on a level with your knees. Keep both feet together and keep your arms straight. *Now* try to jump over the stick – it's very difficult to do it and not fall over; but with practice you'll get the hang of it.

7
Parties for 11s and 12s

Rainbow Party

(3 hours) *Early evening, indoors*

Invitations

Materials
Thin card
Paints/felt tips
Envelopes (different colours if possible)

Fold and cut the card to fit the envelopes. Colour as brightly as possible in rainbow colours: red – orange – yellow – green – blue – indigo – violet.

Write your invitation on the inside (see Chapter 1 for suggested wording), and ask your guests to wear as many different colours as possible. Say that there will be a prize for the 'most colourful' costume.

Make extras for thank you cards.

Decorations

Materials
Coloured streamers
Rainbow balloons
Thin card
Felt tips/paints
String

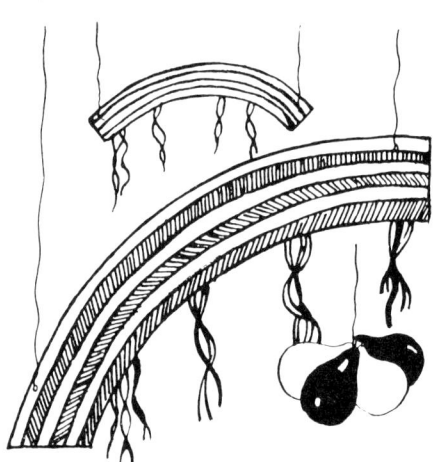

Make rainbows from card, decorate with streamers, and suspend from ceiling. Hang coloured streamers and rainbow balloons around the room.

Cake

Use the rainbow theme in either of the following ways:

Cut a large round cake into a rainbow shape and stand up as shown. Cover in white icing and paint on the colours with food colouring

Keep cake in round shape and cover in blue icing (sky); add a few white clouds. Finish by making a cardboard rainbow and stand it on the top. Write 'Happy Birthday' on the rainbow.

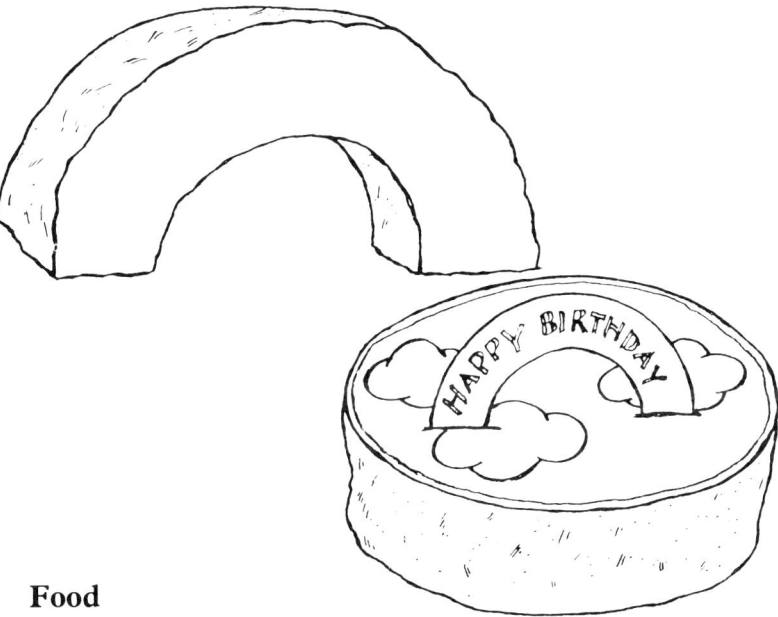

Food

Buffet including 'Fortune Cookies'. Fortunes to be written on paper and wrapped in greaseproof paper or foil. Cook inside any small cakes or biscuits. Alternatively, place inside brandy snaps.

PROGRAMME
Music essential

Games to be played will be interspersed with pop music and dancing.

Ask each guest to bring a favourite record or tape.

Party competition: Who is it?

Props
A baby photograph of each guest
Paper and pencil for each guest
Prize

Number the photographs. Arrange them on a display board or around the room. Give each person a piece of paper and a pencil and ask them to guess which photograph belongs to each guest. Get them to put their names at the top and to hand their completed list to you during the party. Tell them you will give the answers at the end.

Rainbow tissues

Props
Rainbow tissues
Coloured straws
Prize

Divide the players into two teams. Give them a straw each. Place four or five tissues for each team at the 'start' end of the line.

Tell the players they have to pass the tissue down the line without touching it, just using the straw and sucking in or out. If the tissue drops, the player who dropped it is allowed to pick it up again and put it back on the end of his/her straw. Pass all the tissues down the line. Requires a lot of concentration.

The team that gets all its tissues down the line first wins the game.

Musical colours

Props
Music
Coloured streamers or large coloured discs, in several different colours
Prize

Give each player a coloured streamer/disc. Play the music and they dance. When the music stops call a number – 2, 3 or 4. The players have to form pairs or groups of the number called but all the members of each group must be holding streamers or discs of the same colour. Players who cannot fit into a group must drop out. Continue until you have one or two winners.

Shoe fly

Props
A box large enough to hold one shoe from each guest
Prizes
Whistle

Ask each player to take off a shoe and put it in the box. The players then stand in a large circle around it. Ask each player to look at the shoe worn by the person on their right. This is the shoe whose pair they have to find and put on its owner's foot. The winners will be the first one who is wearing a pair of shoes and the 'finder'. Blow the whistle and watch the chaos!

*

Buffet

*

Rainbow parade

The guests parade in their 'party clothes'. Award a small prize for the most colourful display.

Paperclip race

Props
One paperclip for each player
Team prize

Divide players into two teams and sit them facing each other. The players hold the paperclips behind their backs. At a given signal the two leaders pass their clips to the next player in their team – who has to hook it on to her/his own and pass it to the next player, and so on. When the chain has been completed the last player has to place it on his knees, pick it up with his knuckles and drop it on the next one's knees. Continue in this manner until it reaches the leader, who puts it behind her/his back again and unhooks and keeps a clip. (S)he then passes it to the next player who also unhooks a clip. Continue like this right down the line. The winning team is the first one which has all its members holding up their single unhooked paperclips.

Eye witness

Props
An accomplice, dressed in an assortment of clothes, odd gloves, funny hat, bag to carry, rolled-up newspaper, umbrella, one wellie, one shoe etc. Keep him/her out of sight
Pencil and paper for each player

Explain to the guests that there has been a robbery. You think the robber is still around and you have all been asked to give an accurate description should you see her/him. Hand out pencils and paper. When this has been done shout, 'Police' – upon which the robber will come into the room, run around it a couple of times and dash out again.

Ask everyone to write down a description of what the robber was wearing. When they have all completed a list, the robber can come back to judge who has the most accurate description.

Have some more clothes ready in case someone else would like to volunteer to be the robber.

Competition answers

Give each person a list to correct (not their own). Call out 'Number 1'. The person whose picture is Number 1 steps up to take it from the display. Continue until all the photographs have been identified.

Award a prize to the person with the most accurate list.

Bar-B-Q Party
(3 hours) *Outdoors*

Invitations – 'Bangers or Burgers'

Materials
Thin card
Envelopes
Felt tips/paints

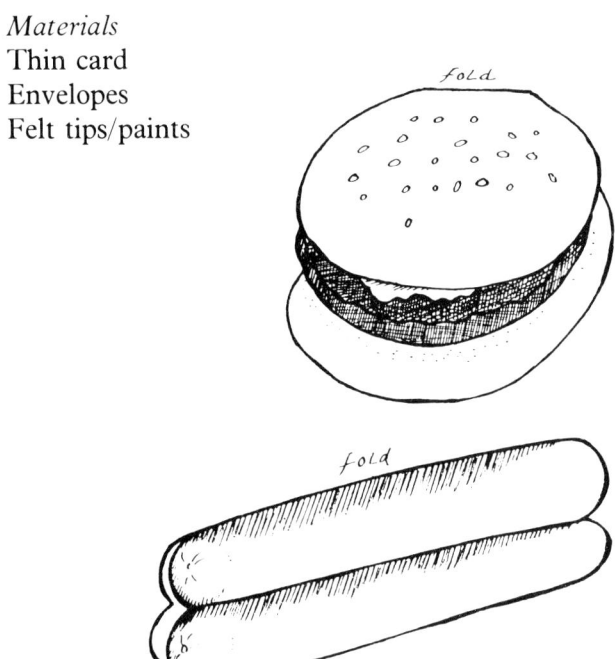

Making sure that it fits the envelope, make a template from paper of either bangers or burgers (whichever will be on the menu) as shown.

Fold the card and, using the template, draw and cut out the invitations. Decorate to look like sausages or burgers. Write your invitation on the inside (see Chapter 1 for suggested wording) and also ask your guests to dress 'Country and Western' style.

Decorations

Streamers, balloons and any bright decorations available; maybe a banner made from an oblong piece of sheet (or similar). Write 'Welcome to the BAR-B-Q' on the banner and hang it up over the entrance.

Cake – 'tin of beans'

Steam the label off a tin of baked beans and put it around a chocolate Swiss roll (or similar-shaped cake).

Food

Bangers, mash and beans, followed by doughnuts. Alternatively, have beefburgers or toasted sandwiches and flapjacks.

PROGRAMME

Music is essential. (It could be set up in the garage or inside an open window.) Ask each guest to bring a record or tape.

The games to be played will be interspersed with music and dancing.

Party competition: 'Best in the West'

Props
Spud gun (maybe a spare one as well)

Cooking pot or large casserole
Potatoes
Post secured in the ground or something to lasso. Draw out a calf's head on a large piece of card and fix on the top

Rope with loop for lasso
Scoreboard (easel and chalk)
Prize: Sheriff's badge and hat with 'The Best in the West' written on it

There are two parts to the competition, which will last throughout the party:

Pot the pot!
Place the cooking pot a suitable distance from the marked 'standing line'. Let each competitor have five goes at shooting a piece of potato from the spud gun into the pot. Mark up the score.

Rope up
Mark a 'standing line' and allow each competitor five tries to lasso the calf. Mark up the score.

Follow the string

Props
Several pieces of string (half as many pieces as there are guests)
 – all the same length and as long as possible
Two prizes

Preparation before the party
Wind each piece of string in and out of things, around things, in and out of trees, bushes and around gates, doors and anywhere else you can. The strings should cross each other at various points, but not be tangled. Make sure you end up with half of the ends in one place and the other half quite a distance away.

On the day
Each player has to hold an end and wind it up until (s)he meets with the player winding from the other end. Then they must wind it all on to one ball. Winners are the first pair with a complete ball of string.

Slap Jack

Props
Rolled-up newspaper (have spares)

'Jack' holds the rolled-up newspaper whilst the rest of the players form a circle, with their hands held open behind their backs. Jack has to walk around the outside of the circle and place the newspaper in someone's hands. This is the signal for that player to chase Jack and try to hit him with it as many times as possible. Jack has to run around the circle until (s)he reaches the vacant place – trying not to get hit. If Jack is hit, (s)he has to continue on the outside. If not, the player holding the newspaper is the new Jack.

Brimming over

Props
4 cups full of water

Divide the players into four teams. Give the first player in each team a paper cup, really brimming over with water. On the word 'Go' the first player runs round to the back of the line, trying not to spill the water. Then the cup is passed back up the line to the new person at the front, who sets off for the back, and the cup is passed forward again. This goes on until the original player is back at the front.

When all the teams are back in their original positions, the winners are the team with the most water left in their cup.

Bar-B-Q

Entertainment: ask each guest to come prepared to perform a stunt, play a trick, tell jokes or sing a song.

Pass the bridle

Props
Bridle, made from rope as shown (two loops for arms, joined across shoulders with two short 'reins' attached)

Cushion (for saddle)
Cowboy hat

Players form a circle and music is played whilst the bridle is passed around. When the music stops the person holding the bridle is the 'horse'. The horse chooses his/her 'rider'; you supply the saddle (cushion). The horse goes on all fours and has the bridle put on him/her, and the cowboy gets a hat. The cowboy sits on the horse, and rides it around the circle – the horse making appropriate whinneying noises. When they have completed a circle, the horse is put back in the stable (back in the circle), and the bridle is passed around again.

Extra fun
Give the horse and rider an obstacle to overcome. The cowboy is allowed to dismount, but must keep hold of the reins. The obstacle could be a tyre to get through, suspended from a branch.

Burst the balloon – challenge

Props
5–6 glasses of water
5–6 dry cracker biscuits
5–6 balloons
Prize

Ask for five or six 'volunteers'. Give each of them a glass of water, a dry cracker biscuit and a balloon. The idea of the game is that the players must drink the glass of water, eat the biscuit and then blow up the balloon until it bursts. The first person to achieve this is the winner. This is harder than it sounds, since the drinking and eating makes the players feel full, and they find it very difficult to burst the balloon.

Competition results

Add up the scores to see who is 'the Best in the West'. Present the prize – a sheriff's badge and hat.

Extra Games and Things to Do

Give and take

Ask each guest to gift wrap an item they no longer want – in fact something they hate owning! They must bring it to the party and take home a similar present in exchange.

When your guests arrive, gather all the parcels together in a sack and at the end of the party let each one pick out a present.

For extra fun, suggest they open them before they leave to find out what exciting things are inside!

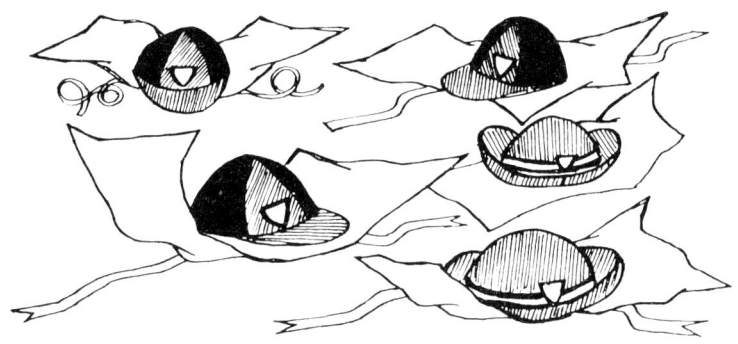

Hanky hockey

Props
A stick for each player
Handkerchief (for ball)
Goal markers
Team prize

Players form into two teams. The object is to score goals by hitting the hanky between the 'posts'.

Don't giggle

Props
Prize

This is a test of control! The one important rule is that it should be played in silence and with a 'deadpan' face.

Ask the players to sit in a circle, close together. A leader starts the game by nudging her neighbour, who nudges his neighbour and so on until it gets back to the leader. The next player chooses a new move, e.g. pulling an ear or making a face, and so on until someone breaks down and giggles, laughs, cries or becomes hysterical and is eliminated. Last one in wins.

Jumble sale

Props
Collection of 'jumble' to fight over: old clothes, old toys, cooking utensils, cushions or pillows, etc.
Score card
Team prize

Form into teams (about six to ten people in each). Make out a list of pieces of jumble, and call out the items on your list one by one. Each team scrambles to get that particular article before anyone else and the team that gets the article receives a point. The team with the most points after a set time is the winning team.

Articles that cause a little fun are two handkerchiefs or socks knotted together, shoelaces tangled up, etc.

Dusty Miller

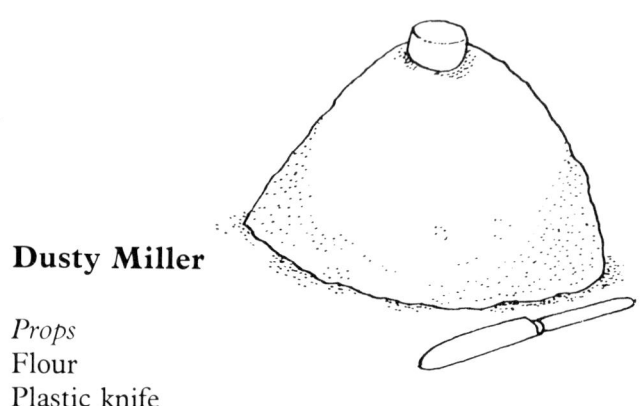

Props
Flour
Plastic knife
Pink marshmallow

Make a mound of flour (by filling a pudding basin with flour and turning it out). Place a pink marshmallow on the top. Place the knife beside it.

The players stand in a circle around the flour and take it in turns to slice off a piece – until the marshmallow is disturbed. The player who causes it to move has to pick it up and eat it without using his/her hands.

Musical statues

Props
Music
Prize

Play music whilst players dance. When the music stops they must stop and stay in that position without moving. Eliminate anyone who moves. If it's difficult to eliminate, tell them to stand on one foot only, or with hands in the air.

8
General Planning and Preparation for Large Parties

Most of the advice given in Chapter 1 is also relevant to larger parties – plus the following extras.

Where?

Indoors in a large hall, or outdoors in a park, field, beach or in the street.

Halls

First find out who owns the hall. It might be a school, church, chapel, council or community. Find out who the caretaker is and make *friends*; quite often a caretaker can make or break your party.

When you have discovered who owns the hall, what do you need to know?

1   How much will it cost?
2   How many are you allowed to invite?
3   How many chairs and tables are there?
4   Can you use the kitchen?
5   Can you use the crockery, cutlery, etc., and will you have to pay extra?
6   Are you allowed to use drawing pins, etc? Is there a piano available?
7   Will you have to take out any extra insurance?
8   What time can you go in to prepare for the party?
9   How much cleaning up and packing away are you expected to do?
10 Are there any 'hidden extras' to pay?
11 In the winter, *check on heating* – like the caretaker, this can make or break the party.

Parks/beaches

Although these are usually public places, it's best to find out from the local council if there are any rules or regulations that you have to adhere to.

Fields

Find out which farmer owns it and obtain his/her permission. Do not stray from the designated area.

Street

Form a committee (made up, for instance, of one from each local club and society) and call a meeting. Choose the street carefully, making sure it has access to toilets, electrical points and somewhere to prepare food. Also make sure it can be by-passed easily. Sunday is a good day to choose, unless the celebration *day* is important. Write to the local council (usually it will be the Highways Department) for permission to close the street. They will normally contact the police, but you will also need to do this.

Decide on numbers and ages (for instance, four to twelve year olds). Have admission only by invitation or ticket. Book indoor accommodation in case of rain. Hire or arrange the loan of trestle tables and chairs from the local town or village hall, school, community centre, etc., remembering that a 2½–3 metre table will seat approximately ten children.

If you can obtain permission from the police and fire brigade, make a 'barricade' of cars across the roads to be closed, bumper to bumper. Make sure five or six are parked next to each other at one end, facing away from the closed street. These can then be moved quickly if there is a fire hazard. Alternatively, ask the police or council for a wooden or rope barricade. Do be certain you are not causing a fire risk – discuss your plans carefully with your local fire brigade.

Draw up a plan of the table arrangements, making sure you have enough room for dancing, games and entertainment.

See also **Street Party** (pages 137–139).

Budget

This is very important, and will decide the cost of tickets, (or not, according to sponsors). Include the cost of disco or live music, throw-away cups and plates, cutlery, hire of tables and chairs, hire of hall, plenty of refuse sacks, cleaning equipment, prizes, decorations, advertising, entertainment, food and drink.

Try for sponsorship. Many building societies, banks and supermarkets will sponsor an event of this kind.

Publicity, and Recording the Event

Make and display posters three or four weeks before the party date.

Local press
Try to get your party written up as a 'feature' instead of paying advertisement rates, but contact the editor *well* in advance. Ask if they will be 'covering' the event and sending a photographer. If not, ask a photographer to come along to record the party.

Think also about a video – to be shown at a later date.

Health and Safety

You may be required by law to insure yourselves against accidents – consult the police and local council. Even if the law does not require it, you could decide it is a wise precaution – get quotes from an insurance broker, or several insurance companies. You may also be able to insure against cancellation.

Look into the possibility of getting a unit from the Red Cross or St John's Ambulance to attend.

Extra safety measures
- If you are in a hall, check *fire exits* and keep clear.
- Locate nearest telephone.
- Ask for contact telephone numbers for the children – just in case!
- Have an adult at *every* exit point.

Food

Think carefully about whether you will make up individual portions, or have everything in large containers. There can be less waste if the children are allowed to choose. Remember also that it's fun (and easier) to have indoor picnics with food in bags (you could even have a Christmas or Easter picnic). No tables to lay, no chairs to find and a lot less washing up!

Celebration cakes

It is a lot simpler to make several smaller cakes, rather than one enormous one.

Amounts of food

An average-sized large sliced loaf, two rounds sandwiched together and cut into four yields about forty-four sandwiches.
About 150 g butter is required to spread thinly over the rounds of one sliced loaf.
To fill the sandwiches made from one loaf try any of these, separately or together

8 medium tomatoes
500 g (1 lb) sliced ham
500 g (1 lb) grated cheese
2 × 250 g (8 oz) tins of flaked fish blended with thick mayonnaise
12 hardboiled eggs mashed with 200 g (6 oz) butter

Cakes can be cut into eight large slices or sixteen smaller ones.

Drink
An 850 ml bottle of squash makes 20–24 diluted drinks.

How much food and drink?

This will vary according to the age of the guests. Here is an average guide: for each child allow 4–6 savouries, 2–3 small sweet items, 1 helping of pudding/sweet, 1 slice of birthday cake and 1 or 2 glasses of drink.

Take with you

Decorations, including string for hanging
Food and drink
Music
Cutlery and crockery if needed
Tables and chairs if needed
Prizes
Black plastic bags – to pick up *all your rubbish*
Cloths for washing and drying
Washing-up liquid
Scissors
Sticky tape and drawing pins

And in case they are not available:
Soap and towels
Toilet rolls
Broom
Dustpan and brush
Potty – you never know!

9
Large Parties for All Occasions

Christmas

COLOUR THEME

Use two of the Christmas colours for the best effect – red, green, white, silver.

Invitations – crackers

Materials
Thin card
Foolscap or similar size envelopes (about 100 × 230 mm)
Paints/felt tips

Make cracker shapes to fit your envelopes. Decorate the front of the cracker in the theme colours, and write the invitation on the reverse side (see Chapter 1 for suggested wording). Remember to add, 'Please wear red and white (or other theme colour) clothes'.

Decorations

Balloons, trimmings, bells and baubles, and other Christmas decorations to match the colour theme.

Name hats

Materials
Crepe paper
Glue

These could be made by the children before the party, and given out as the guests arrive. Write their names on the front.

Place markers – crackers

Materials
Box of crackers

Write the guests' names on the crackers and put in their places.

Cake – cracker

Make from a large Swiss roll (or more than one). Ice it in one of the theme colours and decorate with the other. Make frilled ends from tissue paper.

Food

Choose food and drink in colours to match the theme.

Father Christmas

Many young children are afraid of Father Christmas. If this is so, tell them he will not be coming in – but that they should listen for his 'jingle bells'. He is so busy, he's going to leave his presents outside.

If you don't intend giving the children a present, but would still like Father Christmas to call, ask the parents to provide presents, all worth 50p, wrapped and named. This way every child would have something (s)he really wanted. Alternatively, give each parent the money to buy a present the child really wants.

See also pages 141–2 for action rhymes and song.

Easter

AN EGGS-CELLENT PARTY

Invitations

Materials
Thin card in 'eggy' colours, e.g. cream, beige, yellow
Envelopes
Felt tips and paints

Make a template to fit the envelope. Fold the card, also to fit the envelope, and place the template on it – making sure the folded edge comes where shown. Write on the outside, 'Come to an Eggs-cellent Party'. Fold and write the rest of the invitation on the inside (see Chapter 1 for suggested wording).

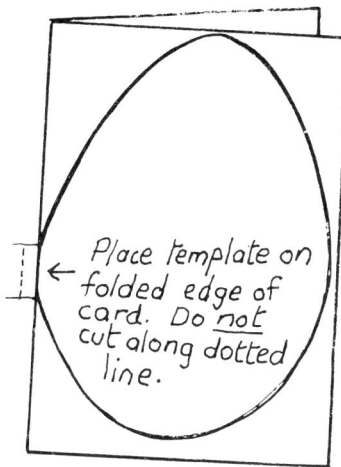 

Decorations

Materials
Thin card
Felt tips
Glitter/ribbon, etc.
Twigs
String
Glue

Cut out lots of eggs in different sizes, and decorate in various ways with the glitter, ribbon and felt tips. Suspend from the ceiling on pieces of string. Hang some around the walls. Bring in some twiggy branches and hang on them either small cut-out card eggs, or chocolate Easter eggs.

Names

Materials
Sticky-back labels
Felt tips

Cut the labels into egg shapes and write a child's name on each.

Place markers

Materials
Thin card
Felt tips

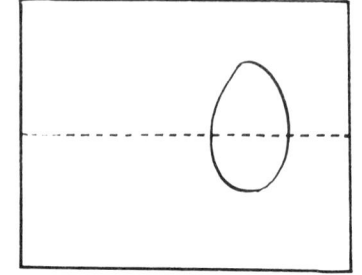

Cut out a piece of card 10 cm square. Mark a half-way line and draw an egg as shown.

Cut around the top half of the egg. Fold over and write on the name.

Cake – 'egg'

Bake two sponge cakes in well-greased pudding basins. Stick them together along the base with fudge or butter icing as shown. Alternatively, use a round cake, iced and decorated with mini egg sweets.

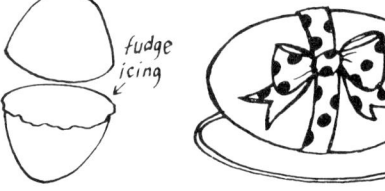

Food

Lots of egg dishes: egg sandwiches, pickled eggs, Scotch eggs. But provide plenty of crisps, non-egg sandwiches, etc., in case some of your guests are not too keen on eggs.

See also pages 141 and 143–4 for games and things to do.

Hallowe'en

COLOUR THEME
Use 'ghostly' colours: black, white, silver.

Invitations – witch's hat

Materials
Black card
White card
Fluorescent felt tips
Glue
Envelope

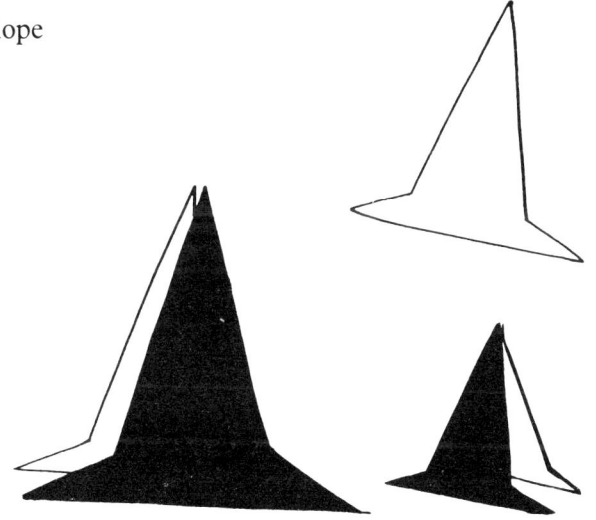

Make a template of the witch's hat, to fit the envelope. Using the template, cut out one black and one white hat for each invitation. Glue the top 1 cm together (black on top). Write the invitation on the inside (see Chapter 1 for suggested wording). Ask your guests to wear black/white or silver and add, 'witches' hats or masks optional'.

Decorations – bats, spiders and silver foil

First the **bats**:

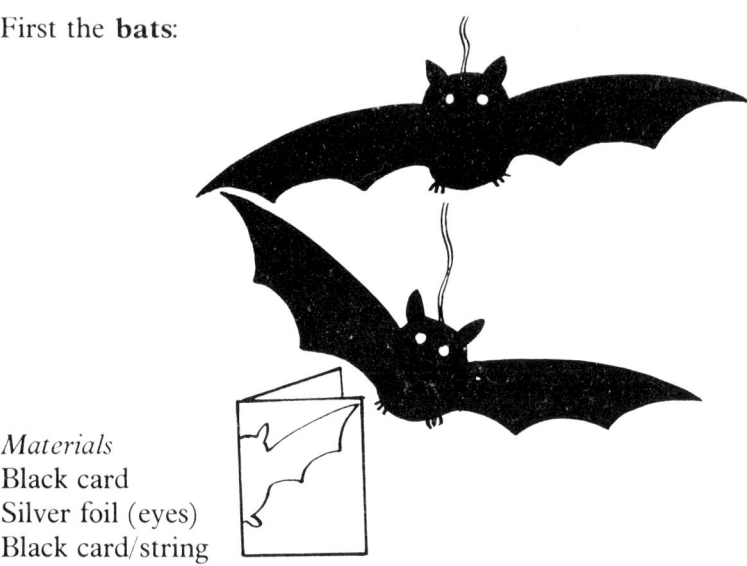

Materials
Black card
Silver foil (eyes)
Black card/string

Cut out bat shapes as shown and suspend from ceiling.

These **spiders** will add a creepy touch:

Materials
Polystyrene balls
Black pipe-cleaners
Black paint
Small screw hooks
Cord/string

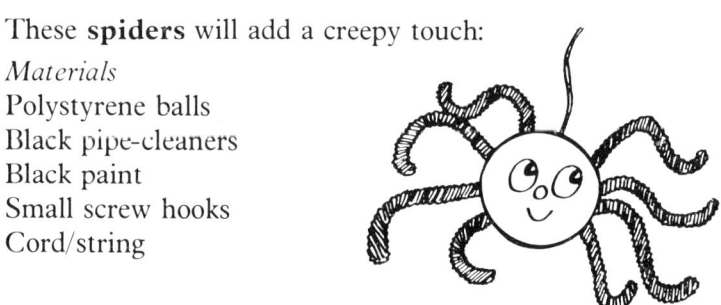

Make eight holes in a ball and push the pipe-cleaners into them. Paint the balls and curl the pipe-cleaners to make the legs. Screw a hook into the top of each ball and thread the cord through. Suspend from ceiling.

These **silver foil** decorations will add the finishing touch:

Materials
Roll of silver cooking foil

Cut into strips and hang from ceiling in between the bats and spiders.

Name badges – spiders

Materials
White card badges (from stationers)
Black card
Glue
Felt tips

Cut out black legs and glue around the badges. Write the name on with black felt tip.

Place markers – ghosts

Materials
White paper napkins
Black felt tip

Fold a white paper napkin as shown. Draw on the ghost's features and a guest's name. Stand up at each child's place.

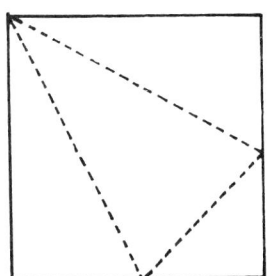

Cake

Round sponge cake iced to look like a spider's web. Buy one or two plastic spiders and place on top.

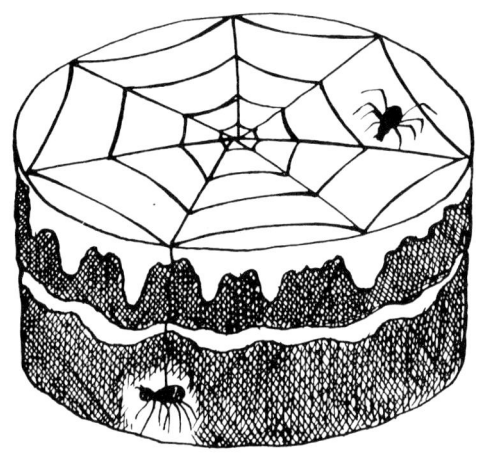

Food

Jacket potatoes, beans, bangers and mash, doughnuts, flapjacks, pancakes.

See also pages 143–4 for games and things to do.

Street Party
(2–2½ hours) *Ages 4–12*

THEME

The particular reason for the celebration will suggest the theme, e.g. jubilee, coronation, etc. You could have a patriotic red, white and blue colour theme, or give it a historical theme to match the period suggested by the event, e.g. Victorian, Twenties or Fifties.

Invitations

By the sale of tickets (price and numbers according to your budget). You could make these, or get them professionally printed or photocopied.

Write clearly on the tickets, and in all publicity: 'Admission by ticket (or invitation) only'.

Decorations

Street bunting, balloons, etc. Sponsors will often provide these.

Stage

If you want a raised area for announcements, performances, judges, etc., use the trailer of a large lorry, and position it near to an electric point.

Table covering

Lining paper or 'Banqueting roll'. Drawing pins to secure.

'Banqueting roll' is a roll (rather like wallpaper roll) of paper used by caterers. You can usually order it from larger stationers, or get it from a cash and carry.

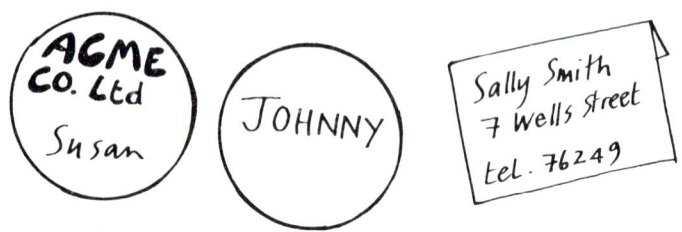

Name badges or identification badges

To enable you to recognize the children at the party and to uncover gate crashers.

Materials
If you have managed to get a sponsor, they may be willing to provide badges. If not, use white, red, or blue badges from stationers.

A good idea for younger guests is to ask the parents to make a badge which includes the child's name and address. (Put this request on the invitation ticket.)

Food

Don't try to be too ambitious. Small sausage rolls for 'cold dogs', small assorted sandwiches, small cakes and biscuits (without wrappings), plenty of crisps/potato rings, etc.

Timing

Make car/wood/rope barricade one hour before the party begins (but see note on page 123). Arrange tables and chairs, put up bunting and pin on table covering.

Helpers

Lots of adults will be needed. Stewards at places of entry to accept tickets and give badges. Someone to act as a Master of Ceremonies: welcoming the guests – and telling them where toilets are situated. People to help with food and drink. Arrange all this well in advance, and make sure everyone knows their job.

PROGRAMME

Competition

Hats or rosettes to be worn to the party and judged during the afternoon by a 'public figure', e.g. the mayor, or sponsors.

Disco music

For everybody to dance.

Hat or rosette parade

Judge the entries, and present the prizes.

Action songs

Have live music for these if possible. Suggestions are *Hokey Cokey* (page 29), *If you're happy and you know it* (page 51), *The Grand Old Duke of York* (page 37); *Old MacDonald* (page 80). There is often a current chart-topper that can be used as an action song!

(Put food on tables during this activity.)

Finish with the 'conga', leading the children to their seats.

*

Tea

*

Punch and Judy and/or display by majorettes/brass band or similar.

Live band or disco to finish

Present to take home?

This will depend on your budget. Party blowers, balloons, pens or pencils, souvenir mugs.

Any Other Time Parties

Hat party
Hat-shaped invitations, name badges and place markers. Everyone must wear a hat.

Space party
Rocket-shaped invitations, name badges and place markers. Fancy dress. Balloon rocket race.

Pirate party
Pirate fancy dress. Pirate's hat or ship-shaped invites, name badges. Ship's food.

Pyjama party
Bed-shaped invites, name badges, place markers. Everyone has to wear pyjamas and bring a favourite cuddly toy.

Bird and butterfly party
Bird/butterfly invitations, name badges, place markers. Everyone must come wearing masks.

Nursery rhyme party
Book-shaped invites and name badges. Nursery rhyme characters for place markers. Fancy dress.

Games and Things to Do

Many of the games in the previous chapters are suitable for large parties. Adapt the games to the theme of the party, for example, *Hunt the Jelly Babies* (page 33) could become *Hunt the Egg*, for an Easter party.

Ask groups of three, four or five children to organize a game each. The games that follow all work well with large numbers – some are suited to special occasions.

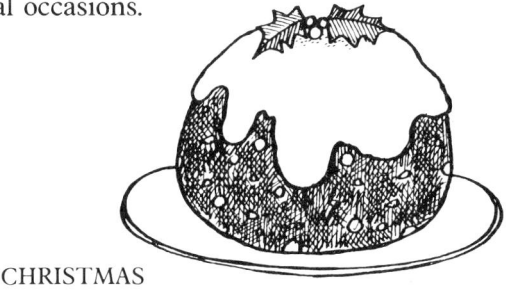

CHRISTMAS

Action rhymes and song for young children.

Christmas pudding

Christmas pudding in my dish,
    (*Pretend you have a dish of pudding.*)
When we eat it make a wish.
    (*First finger on lips and wish.*)
On my spoon, then pop it in.
    (*Pretend to spoon it up and pop into mouth.*)
Chew it; swallow it; give a grin.
    (*Do as rhyme suggests.*)
Down it goes – yummy, yummy –
    (*Hand downwards towards tummy.*)
Round and round in my tummy.
    (*Hand round and round on tummy.*)

Here we go round the Christmas tree

Sing to the tune of *Here we go round the mulberry bush.*

Chorus
Here we go round the Christmas tree,
   (*Children hold hands and circle around throughout chorus.*)
The Christmas tree,
The Christmas tree.
Here we go round the Christmas tree
On a frosty Christmas morning.

Verse
This is the way we jingle bells,
   (*Pretend to ring bells or have real ones.*)
Jingle bells,
Jingle bells.
This is the way we jingle bells
On a frosty Christmas morning.

   (*Circle again singing chorus.*)

Verse
This is the way a cracker goes 'Pop!' ...
   (*Clap hands on the word 'Pop!'. Continue verse and chorus.*)

Verse
This is the way we feed the birds ...
   (*Pretend to feed birds. Continue verse and chorus.*)

Use your own imagination and include other Christmassy verses.

EASTER
Chickens for sale

This is a game for the 5–9 age group, and any number of children may play. All the chickens for sale form a line or circle and the buyer walks along slowly, looking them over carefully.

'I need a plump tender chicken for my pot,' the buyer says, feeling every child's face with his finger. Sometimes (s)he tickles them and says, 'This one looks tough' or 'This one looks skinny'. If the chicken thus addressed laughs, chuckles or even smiles the buyer selects it for the pot, and it moves out of the line (or circle). The buyer continues to test and comment on all the chickens until only one chicken is left.

'It is too tough; let it go back to the farm,' the buyer cries. This chicken is the winner and should be given a small prize.

HALLOWE'EN
Dunking for apples

Apples can be floating in a bowl or bucket of water; or you can have hanging apples, buns or marshmallows suspended on string.

Everyone has to try to get hold of them, using only mouth and teeth, and eat them.

GAMES FOR ANY LARGE PARTY
Musical numbers

Props
Music
Prize

A good game for a large number of people. The children walk, skip or dance to music and when it stops you call out a number. The children have to form themselves into groups of that number. Any group over or under the number is eliminated. Keep them as far apart as possible for the maximum fun.

Beanie
Prop
Bean bag

Someone is chosen to be 'Beanie'. (S)he is given the bean bag, and must go and stand with his/her back towards the others.
Without looking behind, Beanie throws the bean bag over his/her head and the others scramble for it. The one who catches it (or retrieves it) shouts, 'Got it!' Immediately everyone puts their hands behind them and Beanie turns around to try to guess where the bag is.
If Beanie is right (s)he has another turn at throwing the bag, but if not, the one who has it becomes Beanie.

Hares and hounds (park or field)

There should be half as many hares as hounds. Both hounds and hares start running together, then, at a given signal (whistle, loud shout) the hounds turn their backs and count to twenty. Hares can hide or just keep running. Immediately they have reached twenty, the hounds give chase again. The idea is that after a long chase the hares should eventually return to the starting point without being caught. If a hare is caught (s)he joins the hounds.

Letters
Props
Letters of the alphabet inside a bag
Prize

The players are all lined up facing you. The distance away from you will vary according to how long you want the game to last. Shake the bag, pick out a letter, and call it out.
If the letter is either of the child's initials – (s)he takes a jump forward. You then pick out another letter. The first child to reach you is the winner.
Remember to put the letter back and shake the bag each time.